SO-BMX-701

Freedom in Siberia

by Tim Zello

WinePress Publishing **WP** *Mukilteo, WA 98275*

Freedom in Siberia
Copyright © 1996 Tim Zello

Published by WinePress Publishing
PO Box 1406
Mukilteo, WA 98275

Cover by **DENHAM**DESIGN, Everett, WA

All rights reserved. No part of this publication may be re-
produced, stored in a retrieval system or transmitted in any
way by any means, electronic, mechanical, photocopy, re-
cording or otherwise, without the prior permission of the
publisher, except as provided by USA copyright law.

Printed in Canada on recycled paper.

ISBN 1-883893-58-5

To my precious wife, Michelle,
...my very best friend and most treasured gift!
*** Proverbs 31 *******

my mom and dad, Mike and Kay Zello,
the greatest examples of godliness a young man could
ever have.
Through you I have come to know Him. All my
thanks and love!
*** I Corinthians 1:4-9 *******

To the prisoners of Siberia

———————————

CONTENTS

PHOTO INDEX

FOREWORD

The crusade in Amsterdam was drawing to a close. People were streaming down the isles of the auditorium earnestly seeking God. At the conclusion of the service a young man pressed through the crowd, stuck out his hand, and said, "Hi, I'm Tim Zello, you probably don't remember me. I am Mike Zello's youngest son."

"Mike Zello," I responded in surprise and with a wide smile. "Your Mike Zello's boy? I have known your father for many years." He was one of the first workers with David Wilkerson in New York City in the late 50's and had served as the executive director of Teen Challenge in Washington DC for twenty five years. I greeted Tim with a big hug and invited him to join Sonny Arguinzoni (President of Victory Outreach Worldwide) and me in a back room for refreshments.

"Well, Tim, what brings you to Europe?" I asked. He was on the edge of his seat as though waiting for my question, and exploded with a voice charged with excitement and emotion, "for three months I have been in Siberia, Russia..." He related thrilling story after story of God's miraculous guidance and intervention. He explained how supernaturally the door swung open for him to preach in nine Siberian prisons, and what it was like to be the first American to enter many of them.

Tears brimmed in the eyes of this 21-year-old "all American boy" as he described the seemingly hopeless conditions of these former Soviet gulags. Then joy spread across his face as he told us about the hundreds of prisoners who accepted Jesus as their Savior. Sadness again overwhelmed him when he expressed how hard it was to leave his newfound Russian friends.

"I'm going back," he firmly declared, "as soon as I can."

What amazed me was the zeal and passion Tim had to reach people for Jesus Christ. He was totally committed and I had not seen a young person like that for a long time. Later in my hotel room, after we said our good-byes, I thought to myself, "Nicky, you have just witnessed the making of a missionary/evangelist." And I knew Tim Zello was the kind of missionary I wanted to support.

I encourage everyone to read *Freedom in Siberia*. You will be deeply moved and challenged by Tim's commitment and zeal in bringing the gospel of Jesus Christ to the unreached people of the world.

Nicky Cruz

"The Spirit of the Lord is on me because he has anointed me to preach good news to the poor; He has sent me to proclaim freedom for the prisoners and recovery of sight for the blind, to release the oppressed, to proclaim the year of the Lord's favor."

Luke 4:18-19

PREFACE

The following thoughts, prayers, and experiences have been gleaned from a journal I kept while in Siberia. They are the musings of a young man making every effort to "take hold of that for which Christ has taken hold of me." I do not make any claims to be a gifted writer. As a matter of fact, writing is one of my greatest challenges. Perhaps that is why God gave me this task. He continues to show me that the most precious things in life are attained only through commitment, hard work, and discipline. I often wrestled for words to express myself, and as a result some of my descriptions are woefully inadequate. However, the Holy Spirit has compelled me to... "publish with the voice of thanksgiving and tell of all God's wondrous works" (Psalm 26:7). If these pages are of value to you it is because God still uses the lowly and simple.

"O Lord, you have searched me and known me. You know when I sit and when I rise; You perceive my thoughts from afar. You discern my going out and my lying down; you are familiar with all my ways. Before a word is on my tongue you know it completely, O Lord. You hem me in - behind and before; you have laid your hand upon me. Your knowledge is too wonderful for me, too lofty for me to attain. Where can I go from your Spirit? Where can I flee from your presence? If I go up to the

heavens, you are there. If I make my bed in the depths, you are there. If I rise on the wings of the dawn, if I settle on the far side of the sea, even there your hand will guide me, your right hand will hold me fast. If I say, "Surely the darkness will hide me and the light become night around me," even the darkness will not be dark to you; the night will shine like the day, for darkness is as light to you. For you created my inmost being; you knit me together in my mother's womb. I praise you because I am fearfully and wonderfully made; your works are wonderful, I know that full and well. My frame was not hidden from you when I was made in the secret place. When I was woven together in the depths of the earth, your eyes saw my unformed body. All the days ordained for me were written in your book before one of them came to be. How precious to me are your thoughts, O God! How vast is the sum of them! Were I to count them they would outnumber the grains of sand. When I awake I am still with you. Search me, O God, and know my heart; test me and know my anxious thoughts. See if there is any offensive way in me, and lead me in the way everlasting."[1]

As I look back on the last five months I am overwhelmed by the expressions of God's love. The financial provision for my first missions venture was generous beyond my wildest expectation. So many gave—New Life Assembly of God and The Upper Room Fellowship in Maryland; Bethlehem Church, Williamsburg Pentecostal Church, and Ben Torres Ministries in New York; Cathedral of Praise Assembly of God in Virginia; Community Bible Church and North Central Bible College in Minnesota; and Neighborhood Assembly of God in Okinawa, Japan—as well as family and friends; about sixty in all.

"Lord, bless them for their generosity. What can I say but thanks, and what can I do but serve. Take my life and let it be pleasing to You, O Lord. Let the song you gave to me through a friend rule in my heart: 'May the Lamb that was slain receive the rewards for His suffering!' You have named me 'Timothy' that I might honor You. Make me a vessel of honor."

Four days before my scheduled departure for Siberia, a servant of the Lord prophesied during the Wednesday night service at my home church, New Life Assembly of God in Capitol Heights, Maryland. He was a simple man, not well educated and spoke with a distinct Southern accent.

A genuine aura of meekness surrounded him. I don't even remember his name. All I remember is God speaking through a yielded and willing servant. He knew none of us personally, yet I was amazed at the amount of knowledge God gave him about the past, present, and future of so many people in the congregation.

He spoke directly to my parents, who pastor the church. I was sitting in the congregation amazed at what had already been spoken and eager to hear what God was going to say next.

As my parents were standing side by side, the man of God looked at my Mom and said, "I noticed earlier in the back of the sanctuary that you were holding a small child in your arms and I don't know if that was your child or not (actually, it was her grandchild, my sister's son). I don't even know if you and your husband have any children of your own."

He paused for a moment and began again, "Brother and Sister, God is raising you up a son as a 'Timothy' for the work of the ministry."

God was speaking and called me by name! I looked at my parents in utter amazement, and our eyes met, brimming with tears as the prophet continued.

"He has a heart to travel, and evangelize, and a heart to reach out. He will do the work of an evangelist.[2] God will raise up 'Timothy' for the will and the work of the Lord and the power of God to make bare His holy arm, to prove himself strong. He shall go forth, and he shall stand. And he shall fight the giants, and he shall stand. He will not see himself as a grasshopper but he will be taught and know that he is more than a conqueror. And he will not receive the evil report as the rest of them. And he will have a Joshua and Caleb spirit, for God has come to give you another spirit, a different spirit from the rest of the people, so that you will not die with the old generation but come and cross over, leading a new generation into a move of God."

"God will give you a son with the deliverance of Joshua and he shall be the son of your right hand. They shall stand, a Joshua on one side and a Timothy on the other. You shall see the deliverance and the mighty power of God in these two[3] anointed, even in these two young men."

"You shall see the reward of the Lord. 'For I have spoken,' says the Lord. 'I have visited you by dream and by vision. I have not left you without a witness and a deliverance. They shall be used in the ministry. They shall be used mightily to deliver and to reach many and to pull down the gates of hell. And they shall deliver people out of death and bondage,' says the Lord."

God had called me by name! I do not understand why He chose me. But He has. And by his word He has given me strength and faith to go to Siberia to share the Gospel. I know it is His will.

---

1 Psalm 139:1-18,23-24
2 II Tim. 4:5
3 My brother, Mike

Chapter 1

APPREHENDED BY GOD

Tears forced their way through my tightly-shut eyelids. They streamed down my cheeks as the gentle, quiet voice of the Holy Spirit compelled me toward a decision that would change the course of my life forever. For several months I had been asking the Lord to help me hear His voice and obey His call. Now as I sat in chapel service at North Central Bible College in Minneapolis, Minnesota, my heart was pierced as God revealed to me His burden and love for the castaways of the world. The Holy Spirit brought before my mind the millions of people in former Communist countries and how they had been deceived and oppressed for so long. They needed to hear the truth of God's Word. At once, it was as if someone whispered in my ear, "What about you? You can go. You have no debts, no pressing responsibilities, and you are single. I know you don't have the financial resources to give to someone else, but you can go and tell others about Me." A kaleidoscope of thoughts and emotions exploded in my mind then quickly vanished, each one replaced by a pervading, deep-settled peace.

Over the next few months I daily re-lived that experience in chapel. My burden for Russia, particularly the people of Siberia, and my personal conviction to go help them, grew stronger and stronger each time I prayed and read my Bible. I decided not to share my experience with anyone until certain that it was God who spoke to me. When I returned to college for my senior year, the burden became so heavy that I had to share it with someone. I went to a few of my Bible professors, and to my amazement and joy, they were wholeheartedly supportive. They confirmed what had to be God's voice in my ear and His call on my life. I was greatly encouraged!

Sensing a need for additional confirmation, I ventured further, telling my family and several close friends. After the initial shock and exclamations of "Siberia!?", their responses were 100% supportive. However, in all honesty, the affirmation was tinged with sadness and mixed with apprehension, after all, I would be "alone and Siberia was a long way from home!"

Dad suggested that I spend several months overseas before heading for graduate school. He wanted me to test the "call" and to gain experience toward a permanent missions appointment. Having heard of their outstanding ministry of literature distribution in Russia, I sent a resume' to Life Publishers, inquiring about the possibility of a short-term missions assignment. Within two weeks, I received word from Rob Hoskins, vice-president of Life Publishers, that they had an immediate need for help in starting a church in Tyumen, Siberia. He asked me, "Would you be willing to go?"

Well, God had told me to go and the door was swinging open. I knew there could be no turning back.

How does an all-American kid, raised on pizza and McDonalds, prepare for such a mandate from God? I prayed and sought guidance. I contacted friends of our family who were veteran missionaries for advice. I devoured information from books and news articles about Russia, poured over maps and travel guides, and slept on the floor of my dorm room, shunning the familiar, soft bed to condition my body for what I perceived to be the rigors of hardship and adversity. After all, one cannot be certain of what lies ahead...in Siberia!

The price of an airline ticket to the other side of the world plus personal support seemed a formidable sum to raise in just a few short weeks. However, I found that the God who calls, also equips. My home church responded generously, along with several other churches, my family, and a host of friends and relatives. Miraculously, the money was supplied! Donned in cap and gown, I walked across the platform to receive my bachelor of science degree from Bible college. My bags were already packed for Siberia, but only God knew how much I had yet to learn that was not to be found in any of my theology and philosophy books!

Chapter 2

EXCITED BUT EXHAUSTED

To make my flight from Washington to Moscow a little more exciting and interesting, I received word that Life Publishers in Florida was wiring $10,000 in cash to me. I was to take it to Russia for the building of a new church and to support various missionaries. I purchased an extra money belt and boarded the plane with one hundred brand new $100 bills strapped under my shirt which increased the fervency of my mother's prayers for my safety considerably! "Look on the lighter side, Mom," I reassured her. "Now we can be certain someone will be at the airport in Moscow to meet me!"

On the flight from New York to Vienna I sat next to an attractive, middle-aged woman. We introduced ourselves and before the wheels barely lifted from the runway, I discovered she was a believer and attended a Church of God fellowship in Little Rock, Arkansas. She was taking a large tour group to Vienna, Austria. We shared about the Lord throughout the entire trip and encouraged one another in the faith. What a blessing! This "divine encounter" confirmed my direction once again. God always knows what I need, when I need it. As the plane winged its' way toward Siberia, my spirit soared in the joy and peace of complete obedience.

In Vienna we learned the plane had developed an engine problem so, travel-weary, we waited in the terminal for several hours as another plane was prepared for the continued flight to Moscow. Finally I arrived in Russia at 7:50 p.m. (exactly 17 hours from the time I left the U.S.). Exhausted, but excited, adrenaline pumping, I was ready for adventure. The airport itself was quite an experience. Disembarking from the plane, I nearly bumped into a soldier rigidly standing at attention at the entrance of the building I was about to enter.

Later I learned that the Communist party leaders, military, and KGB are pretty much continuing with business as usual except with a different name and with some modification. I proceeded downstairs to have my passport checked at the customs station and was confronted with a sixty foot line of people. Looking around me in the dingy, depressing, and dimly lit corridor, I noticed dust piled half an inch deep on the cylinder-type structure of the gray roof. Choking intermittently in a fog of cigarette smoke, I waited in that line for almost an hour, and then another one for my luggage and equipment.

Little did I know then how much of my time in Russia would be spent "waiting." The Lord was getting me ready for my first major course in the school of missions...*patience*. Thank God all my belongings arrived intact! After clearing customs I walked several yards through another crowd of people holding and waving a collage of signs and placards printed with names. Searching the sea of signs I was happy and relieved to spot a hand-written piece of paper with my name scrawled on it. A young man about my age warmly grabbed my hand and with a strong British accent introduced himself to me as Pete Reed. Pete had been working with Life Publishers for a little over a year and was preparing to return to England, his homeland, the following week.

I waited again, this time on a curbside surrounded by my luggage. Pete had gone to find our car and driver, and about five minutes later he and the driver pulled up in a small Russian-made car. As I eased my weary frame into the back seat, the radio was blaring out a song in English. My heart was grieved to hear the lyrics of American secular music being piped into the airwaves of Moscow, "the devil inside...the devil inside..the devil inside." A rock singer rhythmically belted the beguiling words into the Russian driver's receptive ears. I quickly became aware of how hard Satan is fighting against the kingdom of heaven to make the work of the church more difficult. However, I was encouraged as the Holy Spirit reminded me of the powerful words of I John 4:4, *"Greater is He in me than the one who is in the world."*

Weaving through traffic, we headed south of Moscow toward an office building where Life Publishers is housed in a small two-bedroom apartment. Stateside arrangements were that I stay in Moscow for two or three days to see the city and rest up, then fly to Tyumen, Western Siberia, to assist a young missionary couple in planting a church. But plans had been changed. I was scheduled to leave the following morning, not for Tyumen, but Kemerovo, a city deeper into Siberia. (Thus I entered my second course in missions...*flexibility*.) Fortunately in my preparation, I had read and actually remembered a little bit about Kemerovo, a city of approximately 600,000 people. Peter explained that a team from the U.S. would be arriving in Kemerovo to conduct a youth camp the last week of June and that I was being sent ahead as a forerunner to help set-up and organize the camp. I had no idea of the full extent of my responsibilities, but I was ready for anything God wanted me to do.

I promised to call my parents as soon as I arrived in Moscow but couldn't find a single phone in the airport, and later my attempts to call from the office of Life Publishers proved futile because of bad phone connections. I prayed for God to give them peace concerning my safety so that they could rest that night. Meanwhile, I received a surprise phone call myself! The voice on the line sounded familiar. It was Peter Drake, the Dean of Men from North Central Bible College, where I recently graduated. He and four of my good friends[1] were in Russia for a two week mission's trip. They were in Kemerovo under the auspices of Life Publishers/Affect Destiny distributing the Book of Life[2] in several public schools, had just flown back to Moscow, and in two days were returning to the States. They were calling to encourage me and to say that they would be lifting me up in prayer. It was great to hear from them and heartening to know that I would be able to continue some of the ministry which they were leaving behind.

Before retiring for the evening, I experienced my first taste of Russian hospitality. Helen, an interpreter from Minsk who worked for Life Publishers, busily prepared a dinner of fish soup and buckwheat for Pete and me. The soup tasted pretty good until I noticed that it was full of barnacles. I carefully and discreetly managed to maneuver the crustaceans one by one to the side of the bowl and continued to eat. The soup was complimented by a large crusty loaf of Russian black bread and a small cup of water which had been previously boiled to kill viruses and bacteria. Nourished and content, I collapsed into bed, managing to breathe a short prayer before sleep overcame me.

"Lord, I thank you because you brought me here safely. You continue to burn the desire in my heart for the people of Siberia to know You. Thank you for all the little ways You have encouraged me. Keep me humble and help me to stand firm that I may complete this portion of the battle. Help me, I pray, to bring in the sheaves. Protect me once again as I travel tomorrow and make me a blessing to somebody along the way."

The following morning I woke up at 5 a.m. to discover the sun had already risen. Unable to fall back to sleep due to excitement and the time change I spent the early morning hours with God asking how my life could make a difference for Him. He spoke to me through His Word, "Don't let anyone look down on you because you are young, but *(this is what you do)* set an example for the believers in speech, in life, in love, in faith and in purity. Until I come, devote yourself to the public reading of Scripture, to preaching and to teaching. Do not neglect your gift, which was given you through a prophetic message when the body of elders laid their hands on you. Be diligent in these matters; give yourself wholly to them, so that everyone may see your progress. Watch your life and doctrine closely.

Persevere in them, because if you do, you will save both yourself and your hearers." (I Timothy 4:12-16).

After cleansing the inner man in prayer I went to the washroom to clean the outer man. The water was freezing cold so I settled for washing only my face and hair.

---

1 Zeb Mengutsu, Jeff Johnstone, Tony Nigrelli, & Tommy Orlando
2 A harmonized version of the Four Gospels published by The Bible to All and Life Publishers in cooperation with the Christian Churches of Russia. ©1990 by Living Bible International

Chapter 3

MY MOUTHPIECE

At 9 a.m. Pete arrived and we were on our way to one of Moscow's three domestic airports. Although we were scheduled on the same flight the cost of my one way ticket was $153 dollars and Pete's was only $20 dollars because he paid in rubles (23,000). He carried a humanitarian aid visa which allowed him to pay for airfare at the same cost as the locals. He said that when he came to Russia eight months ago the government was giving out these visas liberally. Recently, they had cracked down on issuing them, so I was unable to get one even though I was doing similar work. Pete arranged to pay rubles for my extra luggage (*JESUS* film, projector, etc.) The total cost was $25 dollars (15,000 rubles and $10 dollars to 'pay off' the baggage handler at his request to "assure that our luggage would safely reach the plane"). Welcome to Russia! If we had paid in U.S. dollars, the cost would have been six times as much!

We were ticketed and our luggage checked in a special section for foreigners where there were no lines, then we were personally escorted to the Aeroflot plane and boarded first. (Foreigners and "wealthy Americans" in particular, are treated well in Russia and in many situations given special privileges). The plane departed on time to Pete's surprise. He explained that delays of hours and even days are the norm.

The plane itself was quite a sight! It must have been at least twenty years old and looked like it hadn't been cleaned once in that period of time. The interior was shoddy with torn carpet and all the furnishings in dilapidated condition. For lunch we were served tea or coffee in old, stained plastic cups, a hard boiled egg, a crusty piece of stale bread, a small slice of fatty sausage wrapped in old plastic, and a few dry, tasteless cookies. It was a far cry from good ole' home cooking, but my stomach accepted the offering and was content. It was God's provision and I was grateful. Little did I know, that due to severe economic depression, I was being served one of the last meals to be offered on Aeroflot. (Future flights included no food service at all).

I was anxious to get to Kemerovo to meet the people God had given me such a burden for. Those precious people who had been in my heart, visions, thoughts, and prayers almost constantly for the previous year.

The plane landed and I was greeted at the airport by Wayne Sawatsky, Yulie, and Yoorey. Wayne was from the United States and had also attended North Central Bible College. Although we didn't know each other at Bible school, it was there in an *Introduction to Missions* class that both of us learned of the great need for pioneer missionaries. Now, God had brought us together on the frontier. Yulie was our head interpreter in Kemerovo, and Yoorey was a student at the University of Kemerovo. His father was the head of medical service in all the prisons of the Kuzbass area of Siberia.

From the airport we traveled by car for nearly an hour to the Motel Kuzbass in Kemerovo. Run by the government, the motel was reserved for foreigners only. It was not a typical American establishment as one might imagine. The rooms were tiny and dirty. Because there were only two motels in the entire city, the Motel Kuzbass was packed with many businessmen from other countries.

My motel bill came to 10,800 rubles a night. This was the equivalent of approximately $8.57. I didn't have time to exchange my U.S. dollars in Moscow where the exchange rate was 1,200 rubles for one U.S. dollar. I wish I had because, unfortunately, in Kemerovo, the exchange rate was only 980 rubles to the dollar.

About an hour after our arrival, Jan Muzart, who was affiliated with Evangelical Bible Translators (E.V.B.) working with Life Publishers came to the Kuzbass to introduce herself. She was accompanied by three Russian friends who were anxious to meet "the new American." Her husband, Eric, was ill at home so I would meet him the following day. As I talked with Jan, the Russians just stared at me, anxiously waiting to be introduced so they could practice using their English skills. Their names were Yorzyha, Inga, and Inya. They had all been taking English courses at the University.

Shaking my hand enthusiastically, they spoke in broken English, "We want to learn about your Jesus and the Bible. We have been attending the Bible studies

29

three times a week." They seemed honored to make my acquaintance.

During our ensuing conversation they told me that many Americans had just come to Kemerovo and were staying at my motel. Misunderstanding them I looked at our group of Americans, counted out loud to "four", and replied curiously, "This is many?"

Inga responded, "No, I mean a lot of Americans." With a strong Russian accent, she slowly continued, "They are from the Seventh Day Adventist Church. They have rented a theater nearby and are holding crusade meetings two times a day for the entire month of June." Inga noticed my look of disappointment and asked, "What is wrong with the Seventh Day Adventists?" The Holy Spirit quickened my spirit as I realized that God was answering my prayer from the night before, "use me to be a blessing in somebody's life."

I explained, "One Sabbath day Jesus was walking through some grain fields, and as his disciples were walking along, they began to pick up some of the heads of grain. The Pharisees told Him that they were breaking the law. But Jesus reminded them that once David, who was the great king of Israel, saw that he and his companions were hungry and in need. So he entered the house of God and took some of the consecrated bread that only the high priest was suppose to eat and gave it to his companions."

Jesus said, "The Sabbath was made for man, not man for the Sabbath."[1] I explained to them how the Seventh Day Adventist church teaches that everyone who does not formally worship on Saturdays (the Sabbath) is disobeying God. "But everyday should be a day of worshipping God, and Jesus is Lord over the Sabbath. He has authority over everything." They received the teaching with thanks before leaving with Jan.

The next day I met Tatianya Gogiliva and Sergei Grechen who were also students at the University of Kemerovo and worked for Life Publishers as interpreters. Sergei was assigned to be my personal interpreter. God gave Aaron to Moses. He gave Sergei to me as my mouthpiece. Sergei was my age, married, and had a four month old son. In a short time we became very close friends. He was the primary person that I poured my life into during my time in Russia. Sergei was with me on the average of ten hours a day. He only saw his son and wife twice in two months.

One day, about a month after my arrival in Kemerovo, Sergei and I were walking with his wife and she asked me, "What is your reason for coming here?"

I responded, "I have come to share with people the good news about Jesus."

In a quiet, gentle voice, with her husband beside her, she said, "If it is for Jesus, Sergei can be away from his family."

Her words touched my heart, and I silently prayed that God would some day provide me with such a woman.

I gave Sergei's wife some children's medicine from America for their son and Sergei a bottle of men's cologne. They were both very happy and responded, "Spaseeba,"—thank you!

---

1 Matthew 12:1-8

Chapter 4

SHOW ME HOW TO LOVE

Wayne Sawatsky was also staying at the Kuzbass motel. He and I had many long conversions and wonderful times of sharing together. Often the Holy Spirit kept us awake all night laboring in prayer, instilling within us a strong desire to serve God and live in obedience to His Word. Jesus sent His disciples out two by two. There was no doubt that God had brought us together.

Not only were the Seventh Day Adventists holding crusades but the Jehovah's Witnesses, Mormons, White Brothers, Hare Krishnas, and New Agers had already been in Kemerovo and established churches. I began to weep on behalf of the Russian people because they have been lied to for so long. They have been without knowledge of the truth and Godly principles for 74 years, and are unable to discern right from wrong. They are easily deceived by whatever religion reaches them first.

The following reflections are copied from my journal during a night of prayer:

O Lord, souls are dying, opportunities are lost, while saints sleep! The need is so urgent and great! Jesus said to "go" and "make disciples." But who will go? Who will work in His harvest field? The Master's harvest field has been neglected far too long. But God is patient and long-suffering, not wanting anyone to perish but everyone to come to repentance.

Who will travail in prayer? I thank God for those who have prayed over me and continue to intercede in my behalf. I truly covet the prayers of the saints and am deeply grateful for their sacrifice of love. Prayer moves mountains!

Who will give? I believe that American Christians are God's primary agency to send out laborers to reap a great end-time harvest. In Russia an American dollar is more than a single day's wages! The investments made in the lives of people are eternal. On that glorious day when we stand before the throne of God these precious souls will be our crown and joy!

I have been reading the biography of missionary-martyr, Jim Elliot. When he was a college student, he wrote: "He is no fool who gives what he cannot keep to gain what he cannot lose." He also wrote about the condition of America: "Their condemnation is written on their bank books and in the dust of their Bible covers. American believers have sold their lives to the service of Mammon, and God has His rightful way of dealing with those who succumb to the spirit of Laodecia."[1]

How often we go out and blow double-digit figures on a meal! But we consider it a burden to invest in feeding souls. May the Spirit of God rekindle in us a holy terror for the One who is able to destroy both body and soul. Too often, Christians give to soothe their conscience. Giving as a substitute for obedience is an affront to God. "To obey is better than sacrifice."[2]

At times I have asked, "Lord, what is required of me to advance Your kingdom?" And I have heard His resounding reply, "Seek and save that which is lost."[3] "God, open up the windows

34

of heaven and help me to see others as You see them and bring them to your salvation."

"Lord, I long to be consecrated for your holy use. Set me apart from the ordinary and consume me with a passion for souls. Open doors of opportunity for me to do your work, doors that no man can close. May I never resist obedience to Your perfect and holy will."

At the age of twenty-one in Siberia, God is revealing to me the rewards of remaining concerned solely with His affairs. He is teaching me what pleases Him. I am filled with gratitude! What great joy it is to be about my Father's business. It is an honor to know that He wants my undivided attention so that I can give Him my undivided love.

The Bible speaks of the "gift of singleness" in 1 Corinthians 7. Is God "gifting" me in this area of my life? For the present time, it appears as though the answer is yes. I know He is teaching me to be content in all things. So, while I am single I will claim this "gift of singleness"—not a gift of passion eliminated but of passion controlled by grace and discipline. It is a gift of complete devotion to God, freedom to do His work, and strength to forbear any prejudice of others for my being single.

God is also helping me to realize that if and when He favors me with a wife, she also must be considered and treated as a gift from Him. She, too, must have found a treasure in singleness and being about her Father's business. He must be her first and greatest love, and her love for me secondary. For only then will she truly love me and be a blessing and not a burden.

Her heart must be one of sacrifice and surrender. One of my greatest fears is marrying a woman who might take advantage of my love and my desire to please her and restrict me from giving my all to Him. "God grant me patience and wisdom as you continue to prepare me for such a serious decision and lifelong commitment. May I take to heart the Apostle Paul's advice to Timo-

thy and 'treat younger women as sisters, with absolute purity' (I Tim 5:2). Lord, show me how to love!"

That night as I was lying in bed staring at the ceiling, my mind wandered back to America and the young woman I began writing to before I left for Siberia. All I knew about her was that her name was Michelle Durochia, she was from Vermont, and a graduate from Zion Bible Institute in Rhode Island. She was also the secretary for the Russian Missions Department and had a burden for Russia. Before I left she faxed me a message and promised to pray for me. I was comforted by the thought as I drifted into a peaceful sleep.

---

1 Shadow of the Almighty, Elizabeth Elliot, Zondervan, 1958
2 I Samuel 15:19
3 Luke 19:10

Chapter 5

LIVING SIMPLY, NOT IN EXCESS

There were only two fairly clean and decent restaurants in Kemerovo. One of them was inside of the Kuzbass motel and the other was down the street. Both were operated and patronized by the Russian Mafia. I only ventured out twice to the restaurant down the street and only then with a group because it was too dangerous to be there alone. The Mafia is a very big problem in Russia. It's leaders and thugs are running the country by threats, theft, and cold-blooded murder. Most of them can be identified by the Addidas sweatsuits they wear.

The menu at the motel restaurant was sparse. It usually consisted of chicken salad, sliced tomatoes/cucumbers, a 'mystery meat', beef, and chicken. (I say "usually" because there were many times when only one of the above was available). The restaurant had two separate dining areas, the upstairs for foreigners and the downstairs for locals. I soon learned that the typical Russian can never eat out at a restaurant without drinking, and they can never drink without getting drunk! This became quite obvious because every time I watched someone leave the restaurant they were staggering, barely making it out the door. It was also obvious when night after night I was awakened by drunkards shouting, laughing, and singing in front of the motel.

Frequently, I was asked, "Would you like Vodka?" I responded with, "No thanks, I don't drink anything that's flammable!" This always drew a lot of smiles and laughs. If I simply said, "I don't drink," they shook their heads in amazement and disbelief, "Everybody drinks!" I also noticed that many of the foreign businessmen at the motel brought Russian women to the Kuzbass for meals and afterwards escorted them upstairs to "spend the night."

Man's heart is deceitful and desperately wicked[1] all over the world. The wealthy desire pleasure. The poor desire wealth. There is a way which seems right to a man, but in the end it leads to death.[2]

I often wondered how the Russian people live off the small salaries they make. The average Russian earns less than $300 American dollars a year. I soon discovered that Russians not only work a regular job, but they also have their own small farm (a "Potcha") which they rely on for food. They live very simply, not in excess. Due to poverty the average Russian family has a maximum of two children. Abortions are common. The average woman has seven abortions in her lifetime.

My second day in Kemerovo I found out that there were five prisons in the city and that Pastor Peter had been to some of them. I knew immediately that God

wanted me to contact him and see if it would be possible for me to show the *JESUS* film and share the
Gospel in all of the city's prisons. He told me that no
American had ever set foot in the prisons of the Kuzbass
region.

The last week of June twenty-two young Americans,
an "Effect Destiny" team from Life Publishers, came
from Florida to conduct a youth camp. They set up in
a large school across the street from the Kuzbass motel.
The camp was held for 200 teenagers between the ages
of fourteen and eighteen. Seven doctors and nineteen
nurses also came and set up clinics in the city for those
who were sick. In the evenings we held Gospel crusades in one of the cities' largest opera houses, which
we rented for five nights (four hours each night) at a
cost of only $114.

I arranged to have the evening crusades advertised
on the radio, T.V., and in the newspaper. It cost only
$90 to put an advertisement on T.V. for four evenings
immediately before the most popular news broadcast.
The radio announced our meetings every morning for
nine days for a mere $25. Wayne had two thousand
flyers and two hundred posters printed for $10. The
city's most popular newspaper gave us four free adver-
tisements. The cost to produce five nights of evange-
listic meetings came to a grand total of $229!

The team from Florida flew in during the first night
of the crusade. While Wayne gave them a brief orienta-
tion, I opened up the first service by showing the *JESUS*
film (a powerful full length movie about Jesus Christ as
portrayed in the gospel of Luke). Approximately one
hundred and fifty people came forward to pray and accept Jesus Christ as their personal Savior after the film.

The majority of Pentecostal churches in Russia are ultra-conservative, traditional, and tend to be legalistic. In most of them the women must have their heads covered and are not permitted to wear make-up. The pastor usually does not acknowledge a person as a Christian or baptize anyone in water unless they publicly confess their sins before him and the congregation.

As a whole, Russian Christians do not evangelize and share the gospel because they believe it is the responsibility of the pastor. They do not express themselves in praise and worship during services as we do in America. There is no clapping in church because during Communism people clapped their hands for party leaders. The congregation ritually repeats the Lord's prayer after the pastor in every service, sometimes two or three times. Many of the pastors have no formal Bible training and little, if any, resources for studying. Misinterpretations of Scripture are common. Also people receive meager portions of the "meat" of the Word, as Sunday's sermons are usually limited to repentance and salvation.

One of my primary objectives was to share the joy of the Lord with believers in the churches I visited and give them hope for the future. The Apostle Paul said, "The kingdom of heaven is righteousness, joy, and peace in the Holy Ghost."[3] The good news of the Gospel is that Jesus has made this possible.

While I was in Kemerovo, there were only two Pentecostal churches in a city of 600,000. Revival Church is a Pentecostal Union church pastored by Stanistlav, a Belorussian missionary, and is registered with the government. The other is an underground church called Biblical Way Church pastored by Peter. Both churches

rent theaters that seat approximately 800 people, however, each had only 40-70 people attending. A typical
Sunday morning service lasted two hours with four
people speaking.

My first Sunday in Siberia I attended Pastor
Stanistlav's church, and he asked me to preach. There
were 114 people attending that morning. It was their
largest crowd ever. Before ministering I was honored to
present Stanistlav with an New International Version
Russian Study Bible and a Russian Bible Dictionary.

The Holy Spirit then led me to speak on prayer and
about the wonderful joy there is in following Jesus. Acts
12:1-16, John 16:23-24, and Romans 8:26 were my texts.
I encouraged everyone to (1) pray to God (2) in the
name of Jesus (3) as the Holy Spirit enables them. The
number one thing Russians (even Christians) lack is
joy! I explained to the people the great joy there is in
living for God. Over fifty-five people came forward and
prayed in response to the altar call. They asked God to
forgive them and joyfully declared their faith in Jesus.

On Mondays, Tuesdays, and Fridays, Eric and Jan
Muzart and I held Bible studies in a room at the University. The primary focus of our teaching was Christian discipleship. On Mondays, the lesson was in English for the Russian students who were fluent in English. On Tuesdays, the study was taught to a small
number of students who spoke French. And on Fridays,
with Sergei interpreting, I taught a Bible study for those
who only knew Russian. The city agreed to let us use
the library free of charge on Saturdays to conduct regu-
lar church services. We thanked God for this open door!

At my first Russian Bible study one of the students
asked, "How can I know that I am forgiven?" I pulled

out my driver's license and said, "How do I know I am allowed to drive? Because my driver's license tells me that I am permitted to drive." I continued, "In America, my parents own a house and they have a deed stating that the house belongs to them. If someone asks, 'How do you know that the house is yours?' My parents reply, 'because we have a contract that says it is ours.' There are two signatures on the contract, my parents signature and the person who sold them the house."

"It is the signatures that make the contract legal. The Bible is God's contract with man. God has signed it with the blood of His son, Jesus Christ, who died on a cross for our sins. However, only one signature on the contract is no good. We can only have God's forgiveness by signing this spiritual contract. How do we sign? By admitting that we have fallen short of God's righteousness and need His forgiveness."

"Once we confess with our mouth that 'Jesus is Lord,' and believe in our heart that God raised Him from the dead[4] the contract becomes legal. You know that you are forgiven because the Bible says so. Jesus said, '*Whoever has been forgiven much loves much.*'[5] Evidence of our forgiveness rests in our love for each other." The students thanked me, expressing gratitude for the illustration.

One Saturday the city library was closed, so Wayne and I decided to take the University students to the park for our Bible study. Pastors Stanistlav and Peter joined us. We brought several hundred copies of the Book of Life to hand out. I ended up passing out all of the books myself, as Wayne played his guitar and sang praise songs. All of the students including the two pastors just sat on the park benches and watched, even after we politely encouraged them to help. Generally speaking, Russians do not interact with other people unless they are good friends. I was not accustomed to this, being raised in a church where evangelism was taught as the responsibility of every believer.

By the time I finished handing out the books, dark storm clouds surrounded the entire park. We all joined in prayer for God to hold back the rain until we had completed our Bible Study. God impressed me to share about obstacles we must overcome in order for God to hear and answer our prayers. Miraculously, the storm clouds did not burst on us. God answered prayer!

---

1 Jeremiah 17:9
2 Proverbs 14:12
3 Romans 14:17,18
4 Romans 10:9
5 Luke 7:47

Chapter 6

JOY AND DISAPPOINTMENT

One evening I was having dinner with Dema, a young man who occasionally volunteered as a part time interpreter. He wanted to introduce me to two of his friends who were waiting outside. I invited him to bring them inside the restaurant to join us for dinner. Surprised at the invitation, he excitedly went out and escorted them in.

They were a young married couple named Alexandra and Ocksanna. Dema asked me to share the Gospel with them. First, we talked about our different cultures and then about our families. After we got to know one another a little bit I told them about Jesus who is the way, the truth, and the life. I said, "Jesus is the Son of God. He came to earth, suffered, and died for our sins so we might have new, abundant and eternal, life. He arose from the dead and has given us the power of His resurrection to live a victorious life."

They sat in rapt attention, listening to the good news for the very first time. "Would you like to pray for God's forgiveness and commit yourselves to live for Him?" I asked. Immediately with utmost sincerity they responded, "Yes, we would like to pray." Right there in the motel restaurant at 11:50 p.m. we joined hands, bowed our heads, and prayed. That night Alexandra and Ocksanna became part of the family of God and all heaven rejoiced. I gave them their first Russian Bible, and they went home glowing from head to toe. They had met Jesus Christ!

There are millions of "Alexandras and Ocksannas" in Russia. The people are hungry for truth. *"But how can they call on the one they have not believed in? And how can they believe in the one of whom they have not heard? And how can they hear without someone preaching to them? And how can they preach unless they are sent?"*[1]

On my second Sunday in Kemerovo I preached at the underground church. Peter was the 25 year old pastor. He had a great heart for God and was wide open to my preaching on needy areas of the church such as joy, praise, tithing, etc. For four months Peter was privileged to attend an inter-denominational Bible college run by an Assemblies of God missionary in Moscow, so he had some Bible training. Many pastors in Russia are very young Christians and some in remote places do not even have a Bible!

I was happy to be able to give Peter a Russian Bible Concordance to help him with his studying and sermon preparation. That morning following my message, six people made decisions to follow Jesus. It was so exciting! Several had tears streaming down their faces as they experienced a new kind of love unlike any they had ever known before, perfect love, God's love! Every Sunday thereafter, when I preached in Peter's church at least three new people visited and accepted Jesus as their personal Lord and Savior. And I will never forget the morning Peter's older brother, who had been on drugs and in and out of prisons, received the Lord into his heart. What rejoicing we shared!

Peter told me that his father had pastored an underground church for thirty years during Communism. I was anxious to meet him and expected him to be a humble man of God. Contrary to what I anticipated, his father came across as bitter, self-righteous, and legalistic. He was deeply rooted in tradition and considered it a mortal sin to clap in church. He seemed envious of his son's education and threatened by his willingness to preach the full Gospel.

One Sunday, Peter invited me to participate in a baptismal service his church was having at a nearby river. Hardly able to contain my joy, I accepted the invitation, and with high hopes, eagerly awaited the following Sunday afternoon excited about my first opportunity to baptize a Russian convert.

When the day arrived Peter's father came to the church, sat on the platform, and took control of the entire service without his son's consent. He told me that I could not participate in the baptismal service. His only explanation was "we do not do things that way here." I think what he meant was, "I don't do things that way here." Disappointed and heartsick, Peter and I gently but fervently appealed to his father, but to no avail.

Once in discouragement Peter had told me, "My father makes ten times as much money as I do, but he does not support our church at all financially." Yet, I could see that with his father present, Peter had no authority. At the conclusion of the service, in order to relieve some of the tension in the air, Peter and I stood before the congregation to explain. Peter said, "Tim and I would like to apologize to you because I had asked him to be a part of our baptismal service today, and I know that many of you would have liked him to baptize you, but the priest (his father who was sitting behind us) told us that it was not the right thing to do."

Peter took a big swallow, pausing for what seemed like an eternity. I continued, "Yes, we apologize on one hand, but on the other hand our intentions are pure and we believe they are good. We believe they are right. It is the heart of God for the church of Russia and the church of America to work together. I long for the day when Peter will come to America and baptize Americans. And I long for the day when I will be allowed to baptize you." Almost everyone in the church came to Peter and me at some point in the day with tears saying that they agreed with us. With grieved hearts and partial smiles, they said to me, "God bless you and thank you."

Why do God's people spend so much time criticizing one another about what we shouldn't be doing and in the meantime neglect what we should be doing? If we are doing what's right we won't have time to do what's wrong! I remember my father telling me as a child, "Son, if you are not part of the solution than you are part of the problem." If we spent as much time praying for each other as we do criticizing one another the world would be a different place.

---

1 Romans 10:14,15

Chapter 7

WINNER OR LOSER?

One of the greatest challenges I faced in Russia was effectively communicating the Gospel to atheists. However, God gave me a strategy and it worked! I asked the person I was witnessing to three questions: *Where did we come from? Why do we exist? Where are we going when we die?* Realizing that these questions were impossible to answer with their limited human knowledge they would become curious and ask me for the answers. I jumped at the opportunity and began telling them what God revealed to me in His Word.

"We came from God," I said. "He created us. Some people believe that we came from nothing or from an atom. But how can something come from nothing? How can all of the matter in the universe come from a single atom? It is impossible! The order and design in nature proves the existence of a Creator. Why can't we see this Creator? Even though we cannot see God, we know He exists. We cannot see wind, yet we know it exists because we see the evidence of wind. We see trees and leaves blowing. We feel the wind ourselves."

"The evidence of God's existence is all around. Look at nature. We cannot see oxygen yet we know that it exists because we exist. We need oxygen in order to exist physically the same way we need God in order to exist spiritually, in order to really live. The reason we know that we came from God is because we have a conscience. We have a spirit within us that is capable of distinguishing good from evil, right from wrong."

"The Bible says we were created in God's image. We were created like Him. Now, does this mean that God is flesh and we look like him? No, God is a spirit. We were created like Him, in that we are rational, emotional, and relational. We are rational. We have the ability to make decisions. We are emotional. We have feelings such as love, joy, anger, and sorrow. We are relational. We have a natural desire to have relationships with other people. We want to love and be loved. God is also rational, emotional, and relational. He desires to have a relationship with us. This brings us to the second question."

"*Why do we exist?* We exist to worship God, to have a relationship with Him, to love Him, and be loved by Him. He desires to have a relationship with us because He created us. However, we have a problem. Our sins separate us from God and keep us from having a relationship with Him. Because of our sins we deserve death. But God loves us so much that He sent us His only son, Jesus Christ, to die for us as a sacrifice for our sins so we could have a relationship with Him and receive eternal life."

"Jesus paid the penalty for our sin with His own blood. He died so we could have new, abundant and eternal life and have a spiritual relationship with God. The Bible says that Jesus not only died but He also arose from the dead. This proves that He was the Son of God. Over 500 people saw him after he had risen and they were witnesses of this historical fact."

"*Where are we going when we die?* Honestly, it all depends on what you believe and how you live your life. You reap what you sow! Like anything else in life, it depends on the decisions you make. If you decide to brush your teeth in the morning, your teeth will be clean. If you decide not to brush your teeth they will be dirty."

"If you decide to believe in God and live for Him now by obeying His word, the Bible, then you will live with Him forever in heaven where He lives and has a place for you. You will have eternal life! If you decide not to believe in God and not to live for Him, then you will reap the consequences of your decision and sins. You will be separated from Him forever and be eternally damned to hell where the Devil and his demons are sent. Some people have asked, 'But how can a loving God send people to hell?' The fact is that God does not send anyone to hell. People send themselves there. Their own sin condemns them."

"But God has provided the way to escape eternal torment in hell through His Son's death. Jesus said, '*I am the Way, the Truth, and the Life. No man comes to the Father except through me.*' So you are faced with a decision. You can either deny the existence of God and live as you please or you can confess to God that you are a sinner, ask His forgiveness, and believe that Jesus came to this earth, died for your sins, and arose from the dead, which He did. But, before you make your decision, I want you to know this. The decision you make has eternal consequences."

If a Russian responded with any hint of faith in the existence of God, I immediately offered to pray with him or her to receive salvation. If in their response they adamantly denied the existence of God, I concluded the conversation with these words, "If you are right and there is no God, no heaven, no hell, and no life after death and I am wrong, I do not lose anything. I still win for I have lived the greatest life I could ever live on this earth. But, if I am right and there is a God, a heaven, a hell, and life after death and you are wrong, you lose everything."

Then I asked if I could pray for God to increase their faith so they could believe in Him. Many Russians prayed with me and became winners instead of losers!

Chapter 8

A BRAVE PASTOR,
A LOST SHEEP, AND
A LOST COIN

Pastor Stanislav invited me to his humble apartment for dinner. It was very small and simply furnished. His wife had prepared a wonderful meal for us. It was obvious that they had given me their very best. We had plenty of food, and cake for dessert. Later he opened his heart and told me what it was like to be a Christian under Communism.

"I was not allowed to teach children about the Bible. I was forbidden to share my faith with other people outside of the church. I could not ask people to repent, even in the church," he said. "The KGB watched our every move. If we were caught telling anyone about Jesus they fined us the equivalent of a month's wages."

"Did you still continue to share your faith?" I asked him.

"Da," (yes), he responded.

"Were you ever caught?," I continued.

"Da, I was fined many times. About five years ago I went to a village to tell them about Jesus. I preached to the entire village in an open air meeting and thirty people wept and came to the Lord. Later some officials found out what had happened. They went to the town, threatening the people that if they confessed to be Christians, the land they farmed would be taken from them." He added, "The farms were their only source of food."

Stanislav then pointed to a black and white photograph of about forty-five people on his wall. It was the congregation in that village. Today they are a thriving, growing body of believers!

In Siberia buses are the primary and cheapest mode of transportation. I bought a bus pass for twenty-nine cents which allowed me unlimited travel for a month. Eventually, I got used to being crammed like a sardine in a bus full of people.

Once, during a bus ride, a man heard Wayne and me talking to Sergei and asked, "Are you American?"

Sergei responded in Russian, "Yes, he is an American pastor."

The man said, "You are the first American I have ever seen." Then he gave me some flowers from a bouquet he was clutching in his hand. I thanked him for the gift and congratulated him on meeting his first American. Wayne leaned over and whispered in my ear, "Don't you want to tell him why you are here?" Praise the Lord for a godly friend, who let the Holy Spirit use him to provoke me to good works!

Gently rebuked and spiritually quickened, I smiled sheepishly, thanked Wayne, and began telling the man why I had come to Kemerovo. I briefly gave him God's plan of salvation. At first he was very interested, but suddenly he hardened his heart and rejected the truth. As we approached his bus stop, he got off muttering bitterly, "You are speaking lies."

The Bible says, *"All we like sheep have gone astray, we have turned every one to his own way..."* Here was one lost sheep that decided to keep on wandering. In spite of his apparent rejection of my message, five other people who were standing near us intently listening and heard the gospel message. Who knows? One day I may meet one of them in heaven, and I still have hope for the man who gave an American flowers, but turned his back on God. I pray that the Good Shepherd who gave his life for the sheep will send someone else along to help bring him into the fold.

Valere, a member of Peter's church, came to the Kuzbass one evening to take Wayne and me, along with Sergei, to a mountainside for a spectacular view of Kemerovo. Valere was forty-five years old and single. He had been divorced for ten years. While he was waiting for us in the lobby (less than five minutes) someone broke into his car and stole his money and driver's license.

The loss was devastating! The stolen money was equivalent to four weeks of his salary, and a driver's license in Russia is not only extremely hard to replace but it is also very expensive. After we took several pictures of the city from the mountain, Valere, although still greatly upset over his loss, made every effort to be hospitable. He brought us to his flat and graciously served us a simple meal of fish soup, coffee, and cookies.

In many Russian Christian homes a prayer is offered before and after the meal. Valere prayed before we ate and asked me to pray afterward. I felt God's love and concern for him flow through me as I prayed, "Lord, thank you for Valere and for his generosity in providing this food. Thank you that he is your child and you love him. Help him not to worry about what was stolen, but let him realize that you know all things and are capable of meeting his every need. Lord, I ask that you perform a miracle on his behalf in Jesus' name. Amen." (So be it!)

When I looked up, tears were brimming in Valere's eyes. I knew that God had touched him and he was desperately hoping for a miracle. I also knew God wanted "me" to be a part of it! He was telling me to give Valere the sum of money that was stolen, along with what it would cost for a new license, kerosene for his car, and the meal.

I had learned enough about Russians to know Valere would never accept money if I tried to give it to him personally, so in private, I asked Sergei to write a note in his language. It simply said,

"Give and it will be given to you. With the measure you give, God will give back to you.[1] *Always remember that God provides for our every need. God bless you!"*

Without Valere noticing, I carefully wrapped the note around the money and placed it on a nightstand in his bedroom. Valere got his miracle, and I got a blessing.

---

1 Luke 6:38

Chapter 9

WOMEN'S PRISON #35

Criminals, political leaders, "enemies of the people," and Christians, most of whom were innocent, often faced exile to the prisons of Siberia. As I stepped aboard the old Russian helicopter excitement filled the air. I was about to embark on a journey to one of these former Soviet gulags. It took a little over an hour to fly to woman's prison #35 in Marinsk, a city 250 kilometers Northeast of Kemerovo. I would be the first American to ever enter this prison, which presently houses over 600 female inmates.

Sergei and I were ushered into a large room with four-hundred women prisoners. It was a very rare occasion for them to see the face of an unfamiliar man, and I was the first American these women had ever seen. With this in mind you can understand why I had their undivided attention as I shared the gospel.

Sergei helped me set up the projector to show the *JESUS* film. While it was playing, I noticed all of the

Tim in front of the helicopter.

prison guards slipping out of the room. Turning to him, I whispered, "All of the guards are gone. We are alone in the dark with four-hundred women prisoners! Do you realize that we could be attacked right now?"

I grinned widely, but Sergei didn't seem to appreciate my sense of humor or the situation.

We managed to get through the film unharmed and I was ready to preach. Choosing the text from John chapter eight, about the woman caught in adultery, I looked out over my captive audience. Lesbians were sharing chairs, sitting between each other's legs, passionately embracing each other. Half of them were more masculine than many men I know. I had never seen such empty, hard-looking women in my life. Many of them were old and had deep scars on there faces and bodies. Others had crude tattoos.

Moved with compassion I began, "This woman was caught in the act. She was guilty. We are all guilty of breaking the law. It is just that not everyone gets caught."

The women burst into laughter.

I continued, "It is true, we are all guilty of sin. But Jesus said, 'I do not condemn you. Go and leave your life of sin.'"

"I don't care if you have murdered someone (many of them had), God still loves you. I don't care if you have stolen a million rubles, God still loves you. I don't care if you have had or are having a homosexual relationship, God still loves you. I do not condemn you, but I will tell you this. Go and leave your life of sin."

"What is sin? Sin is anything you are in bondage to. It is anything that displeases God. Bitterness, hatred, and unforgiveness is sin. Sexual relations with someone of the same sex is unnatural. It is sin!"

"It is our sin that separates us from God. Our sin hurts God and it hurts us. Some of you in this prison are separated from your child. You know what the pain of being separated from your child feels like. You miss seeing their faces, holding them, hugging them, watching them grow, and drying their tears."

Many women looked into my eyes with sad expressions, nodding their heads, assuring me that they lived with this pain.

"Well, you are God's child. He feels the pain of being separated from you. You deserve to die because your sin has separated you from Him, but He loves you so much that He sent Jesus to pay the penalty for your sin. You do not have to be away from God any more."

I continued, "Many people say that there is no God. But I am here to tell you there is a God, and He loves you! I am your evidence. How can you not believe in God? I am only twenty-one years old."

As I mentioned my age, eyes opened wide, and exclamations of shock and disbelief echoed throughout the entire room.

I repeated, "I am a twenty-one year old American male in a women's prison in the middle of Siberia. Who would ever believe it? I am a Christian sharing with you about the love of God and showing a film about the life of Jesus, the only one who can truly set you free! How can you believe there is no God? God sent His Son two thousand years ago, and he sent me here to you today. That is how much God loves you. I am your evidence of His love."

That day over two-hundred women came forward and publicly prayed, receiving God's forgiveness, and accepted Jesus Christ as their Lord and Savior. I can still see the tears streaming down their faces as their lives were being transformed before my very eyes. Hallelujah! Afterwards, I distributed the Book of Life to all the inmates believing that "He who began a good work would be faithful to complete it." They opened their books immediately and began to read about the life of Christ. It was one of the most moving experiences of my life!

Prior to leaving the prison I just had to do one more thing. I shouted to get all of the ladies' attention, "I would like to take advantage of being the only man in a picture with all of you beautiful woman." With that, I received a lot of big smiles, laughs, and a good photograph!

The story continues...

...Two years after going to women's prison #35 a missionary couple serving in Siberia told me that the head of the prison wanted someone to come back. He said that since I left, the women who received Jesus have been meeting on a daily basis praying with one another.

Was it for these forgotten ones in prison that the Lord brought me thousands of miles from home to preach the gospel?

Two days later I met with Colonel Vladimir Ivanovitch Semenyuk and felt God compelling me to ask for permission to enter the men's prisons of the Kuzbass region. I prayed for God to open the doors!

Chapter 10

UNHEARD OF

Colonel Semenyuk is the Director of the Penitentiary Service of the Interior Kemerovo Region Council of Peoples Deputies. He has served in that position for over twenty years and is a former hard-line communist. He is in charge of 20,000 prisoners in the Kusbass region of Siberia. I entered his office and the Colonel sat behind his desk in full dress uniform with all the Communist party insignias still intact. Sergei and I introduced ourselves, and he asked what organization I represented. He wanted to make sure that I was not just an American tourist. I reassured him that I was a representative of Life Publishers and said, "I would like your permission to go to the prisons in this region and show the *JESUS* Film, preach, and distribute the Book of Life. I believe that only the power of God can truly change a man and enable him to live properly in society."

"In America my parents have directed a Christian drug rehabilitation program (Teen Challenge) for over twenty-five years. We have worked a lot with prisons and prisoners who are addicts, alcoholics, murderers, and thieves. The courts allow many of them to be released from prison to come into our program."

"The American government did a survey of Teen Challenge graduates in the 1970's and one recently. They found that government programs had a success rate of only 2% of their graduates remaining totally free from their drug addictions while Teen Challenge had a success rate of 86%. The reason is because we teach them Biblical principles."

"We know that it is not our words or methods that make these men change but it is the power of God and their belief in Him. We have seen first hand the power of God to change lives. I believe that if you allow me to come into the prisons God will use me to help change these men for the better."

I had to explain to him what I would like to do and why. The fact that a Christian missionary from America was interested in visiting his prisons made him suspicious. He had heard about our visit to Marinsk and was very pleased. To my surprise he said, "I realize that religion works to help people and is good for our prisoners."

Then he wanted to see any documents I might have or a letter of invitation from the government and my passport. Unfortunately, I didn't have anything he requested. Wayne had my passport and was at a meeting with the Minister of Health in Kemerovo trying to get me a humanitarian aid visa. I explained this to Col. Semenyuk and immediately tried to change the subject with some name-dropping.

"I have been in contact with German Urjevich Kharkevitch..." (He was the director of all the medical doctors and facilities in the prisons of Western Siberia who had escorted us by helicopter to women's prison #35).

Despite my diversionary tactics, Col. Semenyuk insisted that I needed official documents and an organization (local church) willing to take responsibility for me while I was in the prison. Since I would be the first American to enter these prisons, he feared for my safety. If something were to happen he needed documents absolving him from responsibility.

"I am willing to sign a document releasing the government from any responsibility for my safety," I responded. "Pastor Peter from Biblical Way Church, is willing to take responsibility for my actions while in prison." Pastor Peter was not with me, however, and I had no official letter from him. It was becoming obvious that I was not going to be granted permission.

So all would not be a loss, I asked the Colonel if he had a Bible. He sadly responded, "No." "Have you ever read the Bible?" I curiously asked. He shook his head in disappointment and softly said, "No." "Would you like a Bible?" I asked with a smile. Immediately his face lit up with surprise. Elated, he answered, "Yes, please."

Believing that I would meet him again soon, along with Pastor Peter and the necessary official documents, I replied, "I will bring you a Bible." He smiled, shook my hand enthusiastically, and thanked me. Encouraged by his positive response, I continued, "Has anyone ever told you about God, Jesus, and Christianity?" Again, to my surprise he responded with disappointment, "No, I do not know anything." I replied, "Would you like me to tell you about what we believe?" He enthusiastically answered, "Yes, Please!"

For the next two and a half hours, as Sergei translated, I gave God's great plan of salvation to Colonel Vladimir Seymenyuk. He listened intently as the Holy Spirit helped me recall God's role in creation, the fall of man, the judges, prophets, kings, Jesus' fulfillment of all prophecy, his death, burial, and resurrection, all the way to his second coming. I told the Colonel about God's great love. I told him how "God sent His only Son, Jesus Christ, to pay the penalty for our sins, so we might receive his free gift of eternal life and our relationship with him be restored forever."

After I finished sharing the truth of God's Word, I asked him if he would like to pray for God to forgive him for his sins and receive Jesus as his Lord and Savior. Tears welled up in his eyes. He hesitated a moment, took a deep swallow, and then replied with all sincerity, "Tim, you have touched my heart but for so many years I have been taught that what you are saying is not true. It will take some time, I don't have enough faith to pray yet but you've touched my heart!"

Deeply moved by his response I asked, "May I pray for you?"

"Yes, please," he answered softly.

The Holy Spirit led me to pray for the relationships between the directors of each prison, the guards, and all the prisoners. I remember saying: "Lord, give Col.

Semenyuk wisdom, strength, and love. Thank You for placing him in a position where he can influence so many lives that are rejected by society. Thank You for the genuine concern he has shown for the prisoners. Lord, help the prisoners, guards, and directors of each prison to love and forgive one another."

By faith I continued, "God, I ask that You will use me, the *JESUS* film, and the Books of Life to change the hearts of the prisoners so they will learn to love one another and re-enter society to live productively for You."

After I prayed, Col. Semenyuk slowly raised his head. His eyes filled with tears, he looked at me and said, "Now I know there is a God. I am convinced you are a sincere young man. I regret that I did not tape our conversation and your prayer. I would have made all of my directors and guards listen to it." He continued, "I envy your father. It is obvious that he has invested a lot in you and his deeds have produced good results in you. Can you come to my office at 10 a.m. tomorrow? I will give you permission to go to the prisons. I believe that what you have to say can help us. I will give you the necessary documents and protection to enter our prisons."

"What documents do I need to bring?" I asked.

"You do not need to bring anything, just bring the pastor," he responded.

I smiled and thanked him saying, "I will bring you a Bible tomorrow."

In his excitement he said, "When I get done reading it I'll make my two sons read it as well." He continued to thank me over and over again, gave me several Russian bear hugs, and then had his personal chauffeur take Sergei and me back to the Kuzbass motel. As we were leaving Sergei expressed his amazement saying, "Tim, I have never seen or heard of anything like this happening in my life. Things like this are unheard of in Russia. When things like this happen it makes me believe all the more that there is a God."

As I reminisced over what had occurred that day the Lord brought to mind Psalm 40: 3, 5. *"He put a new song in my mouth, a hymn of praise to our God. Many will see and fear and put their trust in the Lord. Many, O Lord my God, are the wonders you have done. The things you planned for us no one can recount to you; were I to speak and tell them, they would be too many to declare."*

The following day I went back to his office along with Sergei, Pastor Peter, and Egor, a former mafia member and drug addict who had just been baptized at Peter's church. Egor knew many of the men in the prisons because he used to run around with them before he came to Christ so I asked him if he would like to come to the prisons with me and testify. When we arrived at his office, Col. Seymenyuk apologized saying that the director of all the prisons in Russia had just flown in from America, and he had an urgent appointment with him at 10:30 a.m. However, he pointed to a military officer who was sitting in the room and said, "Today he is going to take you to the worst prison in all of Siberia."

I thanked him and we rescheduled our appointment for the following Tuesday. I gave him a full copy of the Russian Bible along with New Testaments for his two sons and wife and a Russian Children's Bible for his grandchild. He expressed his gratitude to me profusely

and promised that on Tuesday he would have some sou-
venirs for me from the prisons. I thanked him once more,
we hugged, and parted.

Chapter 11

MEN'S PRISON #29

As we left with the military officer to go to prison #29, one of the most notorious prisons in Siberia, I didn't know what to expect. On the way we stopped by the motel so I could get my Bible and 100 copies of the Book of Life to give to the prison's employees. During the half-hour drive I told the military officer about Jesus. When we arrived at the prison, I met Col. Vladimir Yakovlevich Arkhepske who had served as the director of prison #29 for thirteen years.

After formal greetings and introductions, we were invited to come back to the prison on the following Saturday to show the *JESUS* Film, preach, and distribute the Book of Life. As Col. Arkhepske showed me around the prison, it was as if I had stepped into the production of a Hollywood movie. All of the men wore horizontal striped, faded gray and black prison clothes (the standard uniform at only the most severe prisons). One man sitting near the entrance had a wooden peg leg propped up on a stool. The prison was crammed with

1,500 inmates. Men from all over Russia were sent here for the worst crimes: murder, rape, and grand theft. They were all at least third and fourth time offenders.

After our tour we had lunch with the Colonel. During the meal, I learned as often before, that I was the first American the Colonel had ever met. He began to talk about his family, and in a grief stricken voice, said that his son, who was my age, had died just three months prior. I expressed my sorrow and gently began telling him of God's love and comfort. "I can hardly comprehend God's love, but you can, because you have experienced the pain that He experienced in the death of His Son," I said.

"God loves you so much that He willingly sent His only Son to die for you! I do not believe it is a coincidence that I am your son's age and am sitting here talking with you right now. God brought me to this prison just for you today." I asked permission to pray for him and his wife. He graciously consented.

Colonel Vladimir Arkhepske and Tim.

As I prayed aloud for God to reveal His wonderful love and comfort them, the entire lunch room came to a hush. His eyes filled with tears as I put my arm around his massive body and said, "While I am in Siberia I will be your 'American' son."

"I will require all the inmates to come watch the film, listen to you preach, and receive the Book of Life," he replied. Then he assured me that he too would come and see the film.

"We will bring our passports on Saturday," I said.

"You do not need your passports because I will be with you!" he replied, smiling proudly.

The next Saturday I arrived at the prison wearing a tie and sportcoat. One of the prisoners looked at me suspiciously and asked, "What is the purpose for a tie? Are you Communist?" I quickly removed my tie, nonchalantly swinging it around like a lasso to show them that they had nothing to fear.

Curious to learn about the living conditions of the prisoners, I asked our escort if he would show me the cells where the prisoners lived, but my request was denied. However, during the presentation of the *JESUS* Film I had an opportunity to speak privately with a couple of the "privileged prisoners" in their living quarters. They were privileged because they were in charge of the club area. I asked them to be totally honest and tell me what prison was really like.

"At this prison six men live in a small cell," one of them said. "The cell is just large enough for one man to walk in between the beds on either side and we are only permitted to go outside of our cell once a week for about an hour or two. Only the most well-behaved inmates are permitted to work in the prison's factory and have freedom to roam about daily inside the prison walls. We can bathe ourselves only once a week. In every cell there is a bucket which serves as a toilet for all six men. Our meals consist of wheat, rye, bread, and water."

One of the prisoners named Mikhail had been arrested for writing anti-Communist poetry and accused of being an "enemy of the people." He had already served twelve years. He gave me a notebook of his poetry. In exchange, I gave him a pen and a pack of chewing gum. When none of the officers were around, the two "privileged prisoners" also gave me a couple of faded gray-striped prison uniforms—two pants, two shirts, and two hats. They were full of dust and fleas.

(I smuggled them out of the prison in my backpack, along with the notebook of poems, placing them underneath my Bible and camera hidden in a case. Sergei took several pictures of me with a few of the prisoners while the officers were in another room.)

The two "privileged prisoners" received Jesus and wanted a photo with Tim.

Mikhail joyfully reading his first Bible.

Men were often sent to solitary confinement and many times without reason. The minimum amount of time they spent in solitary was one month, and the maximum was a year. But in order to legally increase their time, a man would often be put in solitary for a year, let out for twenty-four hours and then thrown back in again.

Little has changed in Siberian prisons since the fall of Communism. Many of the inmates are victims of injustice. They have been forgotten and treated by society as if they are less than human. However, some conditions have improved. For example, men in prison #29 are now allowed to grow hair. Up until 1991, they were all shaved bald. Growing hair may be considered a privilege, but it also presents a problem. All of the men have fleas. I can attest to this because I left the prison with flea bites all over my body!

One major change that has taken place (at least in this prison) since the fall of Communism is that the prisoners are no longer beaten by the guards. During Communism prisoners were often beaten with rubber whips. My two new friends told me that sometimes men were beaten to death.

Another inmate said he was put in prison at the age of seventeen for theft. An older prisoner beat him severely. Desperate to protect himself he killed the man with a piece of metal, and twelve more years were added to his sentence. "They treat us like animals," he said. After the incident he was put in solitary confinement. He said on a different occasion an inmate was murdered in another section of the prison and he got the blame for it. Once again he was put in solitary confinement for three months.

When the *JESUS* film was over, I told the prisoners a story about a little boy who grew up in America.

"There was a young boy named Michael from New York City. He lived a life of pain and fear. His father was an alcoholic, and when he was drunk he severely abused his son verbally and physically. On many occasions he threatened to kill him and even made several attempts at it. Once Michael's father tried to run him over with his car, another time he pulled a knife on him. On Michael's tenth birthday his father hit him without cause, making his face swell, then picked him up and put his head through a glass window."

"The young boy was often cursed at and severely beaten without reason or a word of explanation. Many nights he cried himself to sleep and went to bed with an opened switchblade clutched in his hand. He kept it under his pillow for self-protection because he feared that his father would come in to his bedroom in the middle of the night and beat him. He also kept a dated note under the scarf on the top of his dresser which read, 'If I die tonight my father killed me!' As a result of the abuse, he often fled from his house for safety but always returned because he feared for the safety of his mother and sister whom he loved very much.

"At the age of sixteen, Michael got a job working at a gas station a couple of blocks from his house. This became one of his places of refuge and protection. But little did he realize the place where he felt safe would soon become a place of danger and tragedy."

"A month before Michael's seventeenth birthday, on a damp drizzly day in May, he was filling a flat car tire with air, when suddenly a freak accident occurred. The tire blew up! It was defective. The impact of the explosion threw his body three meters (10 ft.) into the air. It sounded like a bomb blast and was heard throughout the neighborhood."

"People rushed from everywhere to see what happened. Someone called an ambulance and another person called for a Catholic priest from a church nearby. The priest arrived first to find Michael's body (which had bounced off the hood of a car) lying on the wet pavement. He was bleeding to death. The priest administered "last rights" because he believed the teenager was dying. His right arm was broken in three places, and bone was sticking out of his flesh. Every bone in his left hand was broken, and the impact of the explosion had ripped all the flesh off the palm."

"His nose was broken, and pressed flat against his face with the flesh torn open down the right side. His right eyelid and left eyebrow were both ripped open. As a result of the impact, the pupil of his left eye was totally crossed in. Only the white of his eye was visible."

"Michael lay in a coma in a city hospital for four days. During this time the doctors neglected to give him proper care because they believed that he would die regardless of their efforts. But on the fourth day, he miraculously came out of the coma. A private physician who was a customer at the gas station, went to visit Michael and saw how he had been neglected. He had strong words for the doctors and convinced Michael's parents to transfer him to another hospital where he knew they would make an effort to save his life and repair his body."

"At this hospital nurses injected morphine into Michael's body every four hours in an effort to alleviate the excruciating pain. But the drug wore off too quickly. After examining his injuries the doctors considered amputating his left hand (for fear that gangrene would soon set in and threaten his life). However, believing that he was going to die anyway they decided to try and save it so his mother would not have additional grief looking at her son lying in a casket with only one hand."

"Surgeons meticulously operated, resetting all the fractured bones. They put stainless steel pin-like nails through his fingers and left hand. His hand was placed in traction with four pounds of weight attached to ropes and pulleys on the bed pulling on his arm and fingers.

For almost two weeks he lay flat on his back and experienced unbearable and excruciating pain as the morphine wore off. There is an expression in America that says, 'misery likes company.' Well, as Michael lie there on the brink of death, in shock, lonely, with fear and pain, he thought to himself, '*Has anyone ever experienced the kind of pain that I am suffering.*' Then looking with blurred vision at his suspended left hand and feeling the sharp pain from the pins and weights; he remembered sitting in church on Good Friday (the day that God's Son, Jesus Christ died). He remembered hearing about the pain Jesus suffered when the soldiers hammered spike-like nails through His hands and feet. Michael couldn't imagine the pain that Jesus must have endured when the weight of His whole body pulled on the nails as He hung on the cross. He remembered hearing that Jesus died for His sins so that he could be forgiven. Suddenly, he believed that Jesus died so that he could live!"

"Something strange and wonderful happened in Michael's heart. Tears began streaming down his cheeks as he prayed and cried out to God for mercy and to please save him from sin and death. 'God,' he said, 'if you forgive me of my sins and don't let me die, I will live for you the rest of my life.' It was then that Michael accepted Jesus Christ as his personal Savior. From that time on he was strengthened as he remembered the words of the Bible, '*For me to live is Christ!*'[1] He determined then to no longer live for himself but for Jesus Christ, the Son of God."

"Through ten surgeries over a period of seven years God miraculously healed Michael. And he always remembered his vow to God. He went to Bible college where they made a special exception for him to attend because due to the accident he was unable to complete high school and receive a diploma. He married, raised a family, and for over twenty-five years he has directed a Christian drug and alcohol rehabilitation program in Washington D.C."

"God has used this man to bring salvation, healing, and deliverance to thousands of men and women, both young and old, including my own. You see, Michael is my father!"

This was how I introduced myself to the prisoners. As I spoke, you could hear a pin drop. God powerfully used my father's testimony to get their undivided attention and speak directly to their hearts.

---

1 Philippians 1:21

Chapter 12

GOD'S PROTECTION

I returned to the motel and later that evening Wayne and I were in the lobby enjoying hot tea and cookies with our two favorite "babushkas,"[1] when three men approached us. One of them was dressed in a white T-shirt and had short blond hair. His muscular companion had black hair and a mustache, wore a black and white checkered shirt, and was introduced as a wrestler. The third man had on a dark, solid shirt and was either drunk or high on drugs.

In broken English, the man in the white T-shirt asked a peculiar question about the costs of traveling from New York to Cincinnati, then abruptly inquired "What are you doing in Kemerovo?"

"We are Christian missionaries working in the local churches," I replied and also explained my ministry in the prisons. While we were talking Wayne excused himself and slipped away to return a phone call from Yulie.

A few minutes later he came back, visibly shaken. He pulled me aside and whispered, "Tim, Yulie was crying on the phone and she's scared to death! When she and the Muzarts left the motel earlier and were walking to their flat, some men accosted them demanding money. One of them said he had a gun and threatened to kill her. When they insisted that they didn't have any money, he said, 'I know your boss is at the motel, his room number is 428, and he has all the money.'"

Wayne was pretty shook up because 428 was his room, and he had a large sum of Life Publisher's money kept there.

"In our ministry on the streets of Washington D.C. our lives have been threatened many times. God is our protector. If He is for us, who can be against us!" I said, attempting to encourage Wayne as well as reassure myself.

Wayne nodded in agreement with me, but went to find a few of our interpreters just in case we needed help. Meanwhile I went to phone the Muzart's to hear Yulie's story firsthand. Eric answered the phone and repeated the story exactly as Wayne had relayed it, except he added, "The gunman threatened to break into Wayne's room and take all of our money!"

I asked him to describe the men.

"There were three of them," he said.

"What did they look like?" I asked growing suspicious. "So we can recognize them if they come to the motel tonight." As he began to describe the men who accosted them I slowly raised my head and glanced at the three men we had just met in the motel lobby.

84

"It's them!" I whispered.

About that time Wayne reappeared, and I hung up. We had to make a decision. Confront the enemy or spend the rest of our time in Kemerovo in fear. We weighed the odds and figured God was big enough to take care of these guys. With righteous indignation and hearts pounding, we headed for the lobby. Meanwhile, the wrestler had slipped away, leaving the other two.

"What is going on here?" I demanded, speaking directly to the man who knew English.

"I don't know what you mean?" he responded, trying to act innocent.

"We know who you are and what you've just done!" I told him all the information we heard over the phone from the Muzarts.

"I didn't threaten anyone or say anything! It was the other guy. He's downstairs with his wife," he answered.

Tension hung in the air as we waited in silence for his partner to come back up the stairs. Meanwhile, one of the "babushkas" told us that the wife worked as a receptionist at the motel. About five minutes later, hostile and angry, he ascended the stairs. He mumbled a quick apology, and before we could respond, all three men rushed down the stairs and out the door. We never saw them again!

Praise God for his divine protection! Although we assumed the man's wife was a conspirator, we never found out for sure how the wrestler knew Wayne's room number.

---

1 elderly women (who cleaned our hotel rooms)

Chapter 13

DEATH AT THE CAMP

The next weekend, Wayne and I, along with Eric and Jan, took seventeen students from our Bible study at the University on a retreat. We went to a camp on the banks of the Tom'e River. Each of us took turns speaking on various subjects of the Christian faith.

The second night while we were singing Christian songs in Russian, a man in his early thirties stood watching us from the corner of the room. Noticing his interest I went to get him a chair and a Russian New Testament.

He thanked me and stayed for Wayne's entire message on prayer and the Christian's purpose in life. When the meeting was over he introduced himself as Andre, and I invited him to my room. He seemed anxious to talk and asked a lot of questions about God, the Bible, and Christianity. He was clearly distressed and looking for some kind of peace. He admitted that he had used drugs in the past. We talked for over an hour and the moment I was waiting for finally came. Bowing his head and praying with me, Andre confessed his sin aloud and made a sincere personal commitment to follow Jesus.

By the time we said, "Amen," his face was beaming. Exuberant, he thanked me over and over again. I was filled with joy to witness the dramatic change in Andre's countenance. The Spirit of God had truly touched his heart! He gave me a big hug, and smiling broadly left my room with his very first Bible grasped tightly in his right hand.

The next evening I told the students about Andre's conversion and taught on the importance of being a witness and sharing our faith. I read Christ's great commission from Matthew 28, and the parable of the servants with the talents from Luke 19.

"When you meet someone for the very first time and are impressed with them, it is easy to tell a family member or friend about that person. It's natural to tell others about people that we meet. I can't imagine not sharing about the only Person I ever met who died for me. Just the mention of Jesus' name is a witness. In His name alone is power unto salvation," I exhorted.

Six students, both male and female, stood to their feet and made a commitment to witness about Jesus to their families and friends. Afterwards, I was disappointed to hear negative comments and even opposition to my message from the other students. They believed "a young Christian has no business sharing about Jesus." It was as if Satan came in like a flood to steal the Word of God that was just planted. Their resistance was spiritual warfare.

I thought of the time Jesus healed the demoniac and, as he was getting into the boat, the man who had been demon-possessed begged to go with Him. Jesus did not let him but instructed him to go home to his family and tell them what the Lord had done for him and how He had mercy on him. The Bible says the man went away and began to tell in the Decapolis how much Jesus had done for Him. And all the people were amazed (Mark 5:18-20).

The next day, in the late morning, Wayne and I went down to the edge of the river to bathe. As we were laying our towels on the sand, my eye caught a glimpse of what looked like a human sprawled on the hard, rocky bank about fifty yards down river.

"Wayne," I said, "Sergei told me he heard that someone had drowned early this morning." (It suddenly crossed my mind that maybe this was the body of the drowned person). "Surely they would have taken the body away by now."

Wayne and I made a path through the trees and walked over a small hill to the water's edge. We were horrified to find the body of a dead girl on the rocks. Her face was pale white, marked down the side by a trail of dried blood, and covered with flies. She couldn't have been much more than nine or ten years old.

Overwhelmed with nausea and grief, we turned and walked in silence back to the sand where the students had congregated. By the expression on our faces they knew what had happened. They could see the dead girl's body from a distance. With deep pain in my heart and a lump in my throat I uttered soberly, "That is why I shared with you what I did last night. People are dying all around us everyday. We have to tell them about Jesus. It is a matter of life and death."

Although the experience was heart-wrenching, Wayne and I thanked the Lord for confirming my message about the necessity of witnessing. We only hoped that the new Christian students realized the urgency of telling others about their Lord and Savior. Haunted by that scene on the riverbank and a burden for lost souls, I spent the entire night sleepless and in tears.

Chapter 14

LENIN OR JESUS?

On July 11, I got my first opportunity to baptize new Christian converts in Siberia! Pastor Stanislav from the Pentecostal Union church asked Wayne and me to join him in baptizing sixty new believers in the Tom'e river. Pastor Peter and all of the members from the underground church also came to the baptism. It was a great honor and blessing to participate in this wonderful celebration of unity in the body of Christ. Hallelujah! The walls of discord that have hindered growth in God's kingdom are crumbling. They must crumble because it is time to "go forth and possess the land." We can certainly do it! An army divided is defeated. The kingdom of our King is universal. It goes beyond government, denominations, cultures, peoples, traditions, and practices. In Christ we have all things in common, and his love covers a multitude of sins.

One by one they waded into the river, dressed in pure white robes from head to foot. As I plunged these precious Siberian saints under the water of baptism, my heart exploded with praise to God. I was humbled by such a privilege.

60 new believers were baptized in the Tom'e River.

July 16, found me once again aboard an old Aeroflot plane headed for Moscow. I needed to straighten out a problem with my visa. Also, Wayne, Sergei, and I were going to meet an Assemblies of God AIM (Ambassadors In Missions) team consisting of fifty young people from America along with their chaperones. They were flying in from Oklahoma and New Mexico to conduct a children's camp in Tyumen, Siberia. When we landed, Egor was waiting at the airport to greet us.

Egor and his wife, Lena, had come to Moscow on a business venture. Like so many Russians, they struggled daily for a meager existence. Recently, Pastor Peter and his wife had moved in with them and were sharing their one-room rented flat. Egor had been sleeping on the floor so that Lena and their four year old daughter could share the bed. They desperately needed money to get a new flat. The minimum price was a full year's rent in advance. The Holy Spirit impressed me to use some of my personal mission funds to pay their way to Moscow. Here they could buy goods at wholesale to take back to Kemerovo and sell retail. Hopefully Egor would earn enough to take care of his family.

The airport was teeming with Jehovah's Witnesses. Thousands had come to Moscow from all over the world to hold a convention. My heart grieved as I watched them flood the city streets, passing out their deceptive literature filled with false doctrine. The inquisitive Russians were reading "Watchtower" magazine, earnestly searching for something to believe in. My anguished soul cried out, "Oh God, where are your Spirit-filled people who will witness the truth of Jesus Christ and His love for the Russian people?"

After meeting the large group of Americans, a week later, we all flew to Tyumen, where we participated in a pioneer camp for children ages seven to fourteen. All of our interpreters from Kemerovo, Moscow, Minsk, Krasnoyarsk, and Tyumen came to help. The large camp facility was originally built to teach and promote Communism to children. In the center of the campground was a large statue of Lenin's head where the children used to chant praises to Lenin and his Communist doctrine.

One morning when Wayne and I were taking a walk, we were astonished to see most of our interpreters, nearly all of them young Christians, in perfect unity saluting and chanting praises to Communism and Lenin. As a child, each one had participated in pioneer camps in their cities.

Later, one of our interpreters, Svetlana, said to me, "It is hard for me to fully accept Christianity because there are so many similarities to Communism."

"In what ways?" I asked.

"Well, take Christian songs for example, they sound like Communist songs," she explained. "If you take the songs we sang to Lenin, exalting his name, such as 'Praise to Lenin, his name will be forever,' and replace 'Lenin' with the name 'Jesus' it sounds just the same." I told her that all the difference in the world rests in the name, who that person is, and what he represents.

In the evenings, the Russian camp directors allowed us to hold two meetings, one for the younger children and one for the older. It was wonderful to participate in a camp once used by the devil to teach atheism, now being used for the glory of God to teach about His wonderful love and divine truth. About two hundred children enthusiastically accepted Christ and chose to follow Jesus. It was a glorious sight!

I think that I ate every part of a chicken in Tyumen. Each night was a different delicacy...Monday—hearts, Tuesday—necks, Wednesday—livers, and Thursday—gizzards! Just what an American appetite loves most. (I jest, of course.) When there is nothing else, it is amazing what you learn to eat. I ate in faith and thanked God everyday for my health! Throughout Russia some missionaries and workers from Life Publishers were getting food poisoning. A few had been extremely sick, and one almost died. Pete Reed, who was now back in England, told me while he was in Moscow he had a parasite for a month and couldn't retain anything in his body.

One evening during the camp, Rob Hoskins, vice-president of Life Publishers, spoke to the group about the spiritual warfare taking place in Russia. Rob brought to light Satan's tactics. "He is not revealing himself in this country. In most of the world Satan will manifest himself in some way but this is not taking place in Russia. Here his strategy is different. In Russia, for over seventy years people have been told that there is no God, no Devil, no supernatural power. Why would Satan want to reveal himself and blow his cover? Often times the Devil lurks in the very room where the gospel is being shared and his very presence prevents a spiritual breakthrough in the lives of many people. We must plead the blood of Jesus over them and boldly come to God's throne of grace in order to strip the Devil of his control over their minds and cast him out through prayer."

It is true that Russia is thirsty and ready to hear the gospel of Jesus Christ. I could easily write about many thousands of people coming to the Lord, but I do not want to be misleading. Like anywhere else in the world, people are only truly reached when they are discipled one by one. Although many make decisions to accept Jesus Christ in Russia, less than one percent get involved in a church and are being discipled. It takes long term commitment to effectively disciple people.

Chapter 15

THANK YOU FOR COMING

At the children's camp in Tyumen, Rob Hoskins asked me if I would be willing to go to Krasnoyarsk (where he was sending Wayne) for the month of August to work in the prisons. He said, "The doors to the prisons in Krasnoyarsk are wide open and waiting for someone to come." I accepted Rob's offer as God's direction.

We (Eric, Jan, Yulie, Tatyania, Sergei and I) left Tyumen for Kemerovo by train on the world renown Siberian railway. It was quite an experience. Four beds were crammed into a small compartment, and it was filthy and foul-smelling. No wonder they sent prisoners by train, it actually reminded me of the prisons. The train stopped every five kilometers at small villages along the way. It took twenty hours to reach the city of Novosibersk. From there we still had to travel five hours by bus to Kemerovo.

The problem was finding a bus. We waited at the train station for thirteen hours before a bus arrived that would take us to Kemerovo. Totally exhausted, we finally arrived in Kemerovo at five in the morning, thirty-eight hours from the time we left Tyumen.

I spoke at the university Bible study the next Saturday, and at the close of the meeting told the students that I was leaving for Krasnoyarsk. They all asked me when I would be back. "Only God knows," I said.

Sunday morning I preached my final message at Peter's church. With tears of love shining in their eyes, the congregation prayed over me, thanking God for the fellowship we enjoyed with one another and asking him to use me in Krasnoyarsk. Afterwards I presented Peter with a couple of nice neckties and some dress socks. He gave me a big hug, smiled, and said, "While you were gone God provided me with a two-room flat for free. An elderly couple called me and asked if I needed a place to stay. Praise the Lord!"

As I was leaving, an old woman came to me and shook my hand, putting into it a folded piece of paper. I thanked her, slipped it in my pocket, and continued to hug and bid farewell to the rest of the congregation. On my way back to the Kuzbass I pulled the piece of paper out of my pocket. As I unfolded it, four two-hundred ruble notes (eighty cents) fell out into my hand. Tears rolled down my cheeks as I remembered Jesus saying "*the widow gave more than anybody because she gave out of her poverty all she had to live on.*"[1] This loving Russian woman gave to me out of her poverty more than a day's wages. It was a sacrificial gift of love and support that I will never forget!

On Sunday evening I ministered at Stanislav's church. These were my last words to the Pentecostal Union church of Kemerovo.

"God is more willing to bless you than you are willing to be blessed!

God is more willing to love you than you are willing to be loved!

God is more willing to forgive you than you are willing to be forgiven!

God is more willing to comfort you than you are willing to be comforted!

God is more willing to strengthen you than you are willing to be strengthened!

God is more willing to help you than you are willing to be helped!"

After the service, I also gave Pastor Stanislav neckties and some dress socks. I left five thousand gospel tracts that I wrote and had printed in Russian while I was in Kemerovo. An invitation to his church was on the back page of the tract. After the service the people came to me and said, "Thank you for coming. God bless you!"

One woman tightly gripped both my hands in hers and said, "I received the Lord when you showed the *JESUS* film. Thank you so much for coming and telling me about Jesus." Here she was, two months later, happy in the Lord, and attending a Sunday night Bible study!

Another man, 67 years old, came to me and said, "Thank you for coming to Kemerovo. The entire city is grateful that God has sent you here. My wife was not a believer, but after viewing your film about Jesus, God touched her heart, and she began to come to church. He is continuing to touch her heart everyday." He hesitated, sighed, and continued, "When I saw the film I could not help but weep. God bless you for coming with your film and thank you."

The following day, August 2nd, Pastor Peter, Egor, his wife, and daughter met me at the airport to say goodbye and presented me with gifts. After our final hugs, I boarded the plane with Sergei and headed to Krasnoyarsk with mixed emotions but with great anticipation. Following the camp in Tyumen, Wayne had gone to Moscow and St. Petersburg for two weeks to rest and would be joining me in Krasnoyarsk later.

The exchange rate had now dropped 980 rubles to the dollar. I stayed at the Motel Locomotive located inside the sports stadium in the center of the city. My room had a bare, cold, concrete floor, four small metal beds, and a bathroom with a broken toilet. But I was still grateful and ready for God's next assignment.

---

1 Luke 21;1-4

Chapter 16

HOLY GROUND

I spent a lot of time alone in Krasnoyarsk and found myself in a spiritual rut, viewing service for God as mere duty. Jeremiah 17:9 weighed heavily on my mind. I painfully examined my heart and vowed to never say or do anything again in my attempt to serve Him unless it came out of a pure heart of love. Each day I came to realize more and more just how privileged I was to be completely justified by Christ's glorious act of redemption and how unworthy I was to someday meet him face to face. That he chose to love someone like me is truly amazing.

One evening during an especially desolate time, I felt abandoned by God, struggling alone to fulfill a calling far greater than my ability. I missed my family back home and wondered how everyone was doing. I knew they were praying for me. America seemed so far away now. I was in another world vastly different from the one I had known all my life. My thoughts wandered again to Michelle, the young woman from Vermont I had met by fax machine before leaving for Russia. She had described herself as being blonde with blue eyes, and in my loneliness, I wondered what she was like or if we would ever meet. I turned to Psalm 42 and poured out my heart:

> *"As the deer pants for streams of water,*
> *so my soul thirsts for You, O God.*
> *My soul thirsts for God, for the living God.*
> *When can I go and meet with God?*
> *My tears have been my food day and night,*
> *while men say to me all day long,*
> *"Where is your God?"*
> *These things I remember as I pour out my soul:*
> *how I used to go with the multitude,*
> *leading the procession to the house of God,*
> *with shouts of joy and thanksgiving among the festive throng.*
> *Why are you so downcast, O my soul?*
> *Why so disturbed within me?*
> *Put your hope in God, for I will yet praise Him,*
> *my Savior and my God."*

After one week in Krasnoyarsk, God opened a door for me to minister in the prisons. On Sunday, June 8, I entered men's prison #31. Formerly a gulag fortress, it housed fifteen-hundred hard-core criminals. I was thoroughly searched and not permitted to bring anything into the prison but my Bible and copies of the Book of Life.

Six hundred men jammed into the meeting room, and listened to me preach from Galatians 5:22: *"The whole world is a prisoner of sin, so that what was promised, being given through faith in Jesus Christ, might be given to those who believe."*

At the conclusion of the message I gave an altar call. Thirteen men stepped forward, prayed, and publicly accepted Jesus Christ as their Lord and Savior. Their boldness was a powerful witness to fellow prisoners. Afterward the guards gave us permission to have a water baptism service in the bathroom.

In the center of the communal bathroom stood a square tin container full of water just large enough for one man. I stood on the outside of the make-shift baptismal tank. One by one each man climbed in, declared his faith in Christ, and with my hand on his shoulder, dunked him under the water in the name of the Father, Son, and Holy Ghost. No longer prisoners of sin, now they were free to serve Christ with the power He gives to all who believe. In Pastor Peter's church, I had prayed for the privilege to baptize Russians. Never in my wildest dreams did I imagine how God would answer that prayer. A Siberian prison bathroom became holy ground and a tin tub full of cold water more beautiful than the

Tim at men's prison #31.

103

Jordan! I will never forget that glorious day in prison #31!

As I was leaving, one of the men looked me straight in the eye and with all sincerity said, "You are a hero to our entire prison. You are a hero for coming here with your mission. Thank you for coming." He repeated again, "You are a hero." His kindness deeply moved me, but I also sensed the Devil cleverly trying to use those words to appeal to carnal pride and rob me of spiritual joy. Knowing my own heart only to well, I placed my hand on his shoulder and gently said, "Give God the glory! Jesus is the only Hero!"

I love going into Siberian prisons to preach the gospel. People often act surprised by that. They think it is a sacrifice, gutsy, and dangerous. They could never imagine themselves doing such a thing. Maybe I am different because, frankly, I never walk through the doors of a Siberian prison without facing the possibility of death. The most incredible joy I have ever felt is being about the Lord's business, even doing "hard labor" for my Master, and being in the center of His will. It's not a great sacrifice, just simple obedience.

I say with the Apostle Paul, *"That I eagerly expect and hope that I will in no way be ashamed, but will have sufficient courage so that now as always Christ will be exalted in my body, whether by life or by death. For to me, to live is Christ and to die is gain. If I am to go on living in the body, this will mean fruitful labor for me. Yet what shall I choose? I do not know! I am torn between the two: I desire to depart and be with Christ, which is better by far; but it is more necessary...that I remain in the body. Convinced of this, I know I will remain."*[1]

"Enslave me, O Lord, whether it be to a 'madman,' or to 'martyrdom,' Enslave me with abandoned love!"

---

1 Philippians 1:20-25

Chapter 17

"...EVEN IF I KILLED
A MAN?"

On August 15, I was able to go back to prison #31 for several hours. Wayne arrived in Krasnoyarsk three days earlier, so I asked him if he would like to join me in going into the prisons. Prison #31 was Wayne's first prison experience. It was wonderful to have a good brother in Christ with me to provide additional strength and support. I have never felt more drained of energy in my life than after preaching in the prisons.

We showed the *JESUS* film to approximately two hundred inmates. The electricity was weak and running through a thin wire. Several times the projector stopped because of the poor wire and inconsistency of the electric current. In the middle of the viewing one of the guards opened the door, shouted a command, and every prisoner quickly stood at attention and filed out. In a matter of seconds the club room was completely empty. I had no idea what was going on and was discouraged thinking they would not have the opportunity to pray at the conclusion of the movie.

On his way out, one of the prisoners told us the guards were holding a routine check, making sure all of the men were present and accounted for. We watched all 1500 prisoners line up outside as they were counted off one by one. Twenty minutes later they were allowed to come back inside, and we continued the film.

During the second reel, I slipped out and talked with five inmates in a back room. The tiny cell was Volodia's room. He was a 'privileged' prisoner and very artistic. Volodia gave me a beautiful container he had handpainted the night before and signed it for me with an old fountain pen. Another prisoner, Sasha, gave me three prison hats.

Each prison had its own distinct style of hat. Some of the older prisoners who were serving long sentences had extra hats that were handmade. I collected a hat from each prison I visited. In return for their gifts I gave them packages of Starburst candy. With the door closed, I put on some of their prison clothes, set my camera (smuggled in, "Lord forgive me!") on automatic, and snapped a picture with them. I later regretted putting on the uniform because it stirred up the fleas. I was bitten everywhere! After establishing a friendship with the men I introduced them to the only true friend, one who sticks closer than a brother.

Ten minutes later all five men prayed aloud declaring their faith in Jesus and received God's forgiveness for their sins. The oldest of the five had already been in prison ten years for murdering a man. What a joy it was to tell them, "You no longer have to live under guilt and condemnation because of what you have done.

Although you still have to pay the penalty for your sins now in this institution, you do not have to pay the penalty for your sins throughout all eternity."

"Pray every day and read what I have given you (the Book of Life). If you obey what is written in this book, in the Bible, and strive to be like Jesus you will be more and more assured of the fact of your salvation each day. And someday you will be with God forever in heaven. It will be a joy beyond measure!"

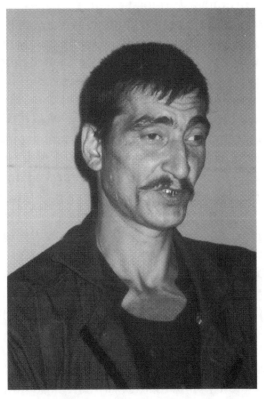

This prisoner received the Lord!

After the movie God once again proved Himself faithful. The presence of Jesus was so real as the Holy Spirit led me to preach about God's love. It was as if the Lord wrapped His arms of love around every prisoner. Five of them had the faith and courage to come forward and accept Jesus before an entire room full of fellow inmates. Unashamedly, they prayed out loud, confessing the name of Jesus and receiving him as their savior.

Later, most of the prisoners came up to me and in typical manner asked me to sign their copy of the Book of Life. While I signed the books several of the men pulled me aside to ask personal questions. One of them was a young prisoner, about my age, named Sergei. With his head down, he peered up into my eyes longing for help, wanting hope, partially afraid, and very sincere. "Will God still forgive me," he softly asked while tears welled up in his eyes, "even if I've killed a man?"

Immediately, the Holy Spirit began to sovereignly move. Spoken words were unnecessary. The Lord was at work! Within a couple of minutes Sergei, a broken young man, prayed out loud, and marvelously received God's love and forgiveness His prayer was followed by a sincere "thank you" and a strong hug. I glanced at my watch and suddenly realized that it was time to leave because we were scheduled to be at another prison at 3:00 p.m.. So with prisoners huddled all around me I said, "My friends, I am really sorry but I have to go." I could see the disappointment on their faces.

As I was leaving the building a pathetic old man pulled me by the arm and asked if I would pray with him to receive Jesus. "Please," he said, "I want to pray a sinner's prayer." We earnestly prayed and he received salvation! I later learned that he had five children and had murdered his wife.

As I drew near the exit to the prison gate, another young man came up to me and asked if I would pray with him to receive the Lord. As we were walking I prayed with him, and he too accepted Christ. Many of prisoners were afraid to stand before their peers and pray, but Holy Spirit conviction was at work as they came privately and accepted Jesus Christ as their personal Lord and Savior. I prayed that during the night the Holy Spirit would bring to their remembrance all that the men had heard about the Lord and that He would soften the hearts of those who had chosen not to believe.

An officer from prison #31 was outside the prison gate in his car and agreed to take us to prison #6. During the half hour drive, Wayne and I shared the gospel with him. He told us he did not believe in God but that his wife and children were Christians. When we arrived at our destination we gave him a Book of Life and said, "We would not be surprised if God sent us to this prison just for you, so you could hear about Jesus." He did not charge us for the ride.

Fifteen minutes later we were refused entrance to the prison, the reason given that no official had notified them in advance. The sealed and signed letter of invitation I had from the head prison director of the Krasnoyarsk region wouldn't persuade them. This was not the first time I had been denied entrance. By now I had grown accustomed to the fact that nothing is for certain in Russia. Although we were not allowed in, we left rejoicing, believing that it was the Lord's guidance, and possibly even his "protection." We were also thankful that He had ordered our steps by allowing us to witness to the officer.

Начальнику учреждения УП/288
тов._____

В августе текущего года по приглашению Союза Х В Е в городе Красноярске находится предстовитель американской миссии "Лайф Паблишен" Т.Зелло,который обратился в СИД и СР с просьбой о предоставлении ему возможности посещения ИТУ края для проведения мероприятий:
    -показ художественного фильма "Иисус"
    -распростронение среди осужденных религиозной литературы
    -проповеди
Положительно рассмотрев просьбу господина Зелло рекомендую Вам организовать для осужденных мероприятия воспитательного характера с его участием.
    ИТК-6   15,22,29 августа с 15 часов.
    ИТК-7   11,18,25 августа с 18 часов.
    ИТК-18   17,24,31 августа с 14 часов.
    ИТК-27   22   августа с 11 часов.
    ИТК-31   15,29   августа с 11 часов.
Возможно присутствие с ним переводчика и сопровождающих лиц из членов Красноярской христианской миссии (2-3 человека).
    Прошу принять меры к обеспечению безопасности при посещении Вашего учреждения господином Зелло и сопровождающими его лицами.

            Начальник СИД и СР УВД
            полковник вн.службы   Б.Н.Логинов

*Official document of permission allowing Tim entrance into the Siberian prison's of the Krasnoyarsk territory. * Translation on opposite page.*

To the Head of the prison   Yr./288
Tob._____

In August, 1993, we are having the representative of the American Mission "Life Publishers," T. Zello in Krasnoyarsk, who has been invited by the Union of Christians of the Evangelical Faith. He has applied to the Home Affairs Department, Prison Division, for granting him the opportunity to visit prisons of the Krasnoyarsk territory with the following purpose:
-to show the film "Jesus"
-to distribute religious literature
-to preach
Having considered the application of Mr. Zello I order you to organize meetings with his participation for the purpose of improving the disposition of the prisoners.

Prison # 6	August 15, 22, 29	3:00 P.M.
Prison # 7	August 11, 18, 25	6:00 P.M.
Prison # 18	August 17, 24, 31	2:00 P.M.
Prison # 27	August 22	11:00 A.M.
Prison # 31	August 15,29	11:00 A.M.

It is quite possible for him to have an interpreter and members from the Krasnoyarsk Mission accompanying him (2-3 only).

I ask you to take measures for providing the security of Mr. Zello and those who accompany him while visiting your prison.

The Head of Prison Division, of the Home Affairs Department Colonel Loginov B.N.

Sealed and Signed

Chapter 18

PRISON HOSPITAL #18

On August 17, by faith, I asked Wayne to come with me to prison hospital #18, hoping they would allow him to enter. Officially, the only American who was allowed entrance to the prisons was the one with an official invitation and document from Col. Loginov, the Head of the Prisons of the Krasnoyarsk territory. The week before I had tried to visit this prison hospital and they wouldn't even let me enter.

Three Russian brothers in Christ accompanied us, one was a Baptist and the other two were from the Vineyard Church in Krasnoyarsk. Outside the prison walls we prayed for God to touch the officer's heart who had the authority to let us in.

While Wayne and the others waited in the front of the building, Irene, our interpreter and I met with Major Sergei Michalovich Kozhuhovsky, the Assistant Medical Doctor of the Prison Hospital. He described the institution to me and said, "This is the largest prison hospital in the former Soviet Union and men from various degrees of prisons all over Russia are sent here. We have 1,240 beds." We talked casually for about five minutes, and then I presented him with several small gifts from America. He thanked me. God honored our prayers, and the entire group was allowed to enter. About 100 inmates gathered in the meeting room to hear us minister.

Wayne and I had become close friends and enjoyed many hours singing together. We opened the service with several praise and worship songs. I asked the men to stand and clap their hands while we sang. There was an immediate rapport and genuine response. The very presence of God descended into our midst, replacing the dark atmosphere of the prison room with an infusion of heavenly light. Wayne preached a powerful message as the Holy Spirit's anointing continued to flow. When he gave the altar call, one by one, thirty men got up from their seats and came forward. They prayed aloud asking Jesus to become Lord of their lives. As the words of commitment, spoken in English and repeated in Russian, reverberated in the air, I felt the triumphant victory of light over darkness and life over death!

When the men returned to their seats I asked all of them to introduce themselves by shouting their name out as loud as they could on the count of three. I counted in Russian, and they shouted their names in unison at the top of their lungs, then everyone burst out laughing. It was exciting to actually feel the oppression lift as they experienced fun, joy, and freedom in the presence of the Lord. We gave each of them a Book of Life. Before leaving, we joined hands in a circle, and thanked God for revealing Himself to us, for pouring out His love, and giving us eternal life.

*Two men dying of Aids at prison hospital
#18.*

In my room that evening, the following words seemed to leap from the pages of my Bible, *"Give thanks to the Lord, for He is good; His love endures forever. Let the redeemed of the Lord say this—those He redeemed from the hand of the foe, those He gathered from the lands, from the east and west, from the north and south. Some sat in darkness and deepest gloom, prisoners suffering from iron chains, for they had rebelled against the words of God and despised the counsel of the Most High. So He subjected them to bitter labor; they stumbled, and there was no one to help."*

"Then they cried to the Lord in their trouble, and He saved them from their distress. He brought them out of darkness and

the deepest gloom and broke away their chains. Let them give thanks to the Lord for His unfailing love and His wonderful deeds for men, for He breaks down gates of bronze and cuts through bars of iron."[1]

God had fulfilled his word that day in Prison #18.

1 Psallm 107:1-3,10-16

Chapter 19

THE "SEVERE" REGIME

August 19, found me along with two Russian Baptists, in prison #7, located in a small Siberian village called Ariysk. One of the guards told me there are four levels of Siberian prisons, each measured by the type and amount of crime. The levels are called regimes. Level one is called *general* regime for first time offenders of mild crimes: fighting, petty theft, robbery, begging, etc. The second level is called *strengthened* regime for first time offenders of harsh crimes: rape, murder, armed robbery, grand theft, etc. The third level is called *severe* regime for second or third time offenders. The fourth level is called *special* regime where the inmates are the most dangerous and wear striped faded gray uniforms. These men have committed at least their third or fourth severe offense. Most of the nearly one thousand prisons in Siberia have 1500 inmates. Prison #7 was a *severe* regime.

One of the Baptist brothers played his guitar and sang at the beginning of the service. He introduced me and as I approached the podium, he whispered, "Don't preach an evangelical message. All of the prisoners in this room are already Christians."

What could I possibly say to these men who had probably suffered more than I ever will in a lifetime? I felt like Paul when he said, "*I claimed to know nothing while I was among you except Christ and Him crucified.*"[1] God proved Himself faithful once again as He gave me words on rejoicing in suffering. In all my life, I have never enjoyed being used of God more than when I was with these fellow members of His glorious church living out their Christianity in dreadful conditions.

There is no way to adequately describe the oppression that is in these prisons. The only two words I can think of are, "NO HOPE." After the meeting I asked one of the men if prison life was a little better since the changing of the government.

"Some things have become better, some worse. We are allowed to listen to music now, play volleyball and football,[2] and sometimes watch TV," he explained.

"What has gotten worse?" I asked.

Lowering his head in humiliation he replied, "They beat us more than what they used to."

"Why?" I asked. What do you do wrong?"

"We don't have to do anything wrong. Sometimes the guards will just pick someone out and beat him in front of everybody. With the change in government the guards have taken more liberty to beat us."

118

A prison guard.

I tried to encourage the men by telling them that they could relate more to Jesus than I could because He too was thrown in prison and severely beaten without cause. "He suffered so that we do not have to suffer forever. And now he is preparing a place for us to live with Him for eternity in heaven," I said.

We passed out Books of Life, signing them for the ones who asked. Then I talked personally to some of the men for over an hour. One of them removed a metal crucifix that he had made by hand from around his neck and carefully placed it around mine. I choked with emotion as I saw the deep gratitude and humility mirrored in his eyes. On the back of the cross were the Russian words, спасц ц сохранц, translated into English it means "save and keep."

Later, exhausted from ministry, we were walking a dirt road to catch a train back to the city. After hiking a couple of miles we realized that we were going to miss our train by about ten minutes. Not knowing what to do or how to get back to Krasnoyarsk, we just kept walking. Suddenly a car appeared from nowhere, pulled alongside us, and stopped. The driver was returning from his *"dotcha"* in the country. Without hesitation, he offered to take us back to the city. In Russia it is very easy to catch a lift because just about everyone who is fortunate to have a car usually needs extra money. The Russian Baptists introduced me as an American missionary and told the driver about our ministry at the prison. After driving us forty-five minutes he refused to take any money. He said God had touched his heart.

That night I lay in my narrow motel bed fingering the metal cross around my neck. Silently and reverently I vowed to wear it always as a reminder of the One who "saves and keeps" and of the man who gave it to me. It represented every prisoner I met in Siberia.

---

1 I Corinthians 2:1-5
2 American soccer

Chapter 20

"THE DOCTOR
OF SOULS"

Irene, one of our interpreters, invited Wayne and me to her *"dotcha"* in the country for a day of rest and relaxation. We hiked deep into the Siberian forest hunting for mushrooms and were amazed at the many varieties we found. I emerged from the dense woods looking like a mummy with cobwebs wrapped around my entire body. We picked fresh carrots, cucumbers, raspberries, and black currents from her fertile garden. Lunch was a delightful summer feast.

A woman from the *"dotcha"* next door told us that if we would like to have a meeting later she would invite all of the people from the area to come. So, at 6 p.m., we conducted an open air service in a small clearing surrounded by beautiful birch trees. Everyone sat in a circle on tree stumps, logs, and rustic handmade chairs as Wayne and I ministered the Gospel. While we were singing, more and more men, women, and children kept coming. It reminded me of the multitudes gathering around Jesus at the Sea of Galilee. They were so grateful to hear about God's love for them and how they could be saved and have eternal life. Watching them all bow their heads in prayer as they accepted Jesus as their Lord and Savior was truly a wonderful sight. With nothing but the wide expanse of the northern sky above us, I could almost see God's smile and hear the angels rejoicing in heaven!

The following morning, Wayne and I went to prison #27, where nine men accepted Jesus. From there we went to women's prison #22 and showed the *JESUS* film. I had to leave during the movie to go to men's prison #6, so Wayne stayed behind to conclude the meeting. Prison #6 was a *severe* regime. I preached, gave a simple altar call, and over fifty men stood up to receive Jesus Christ into their lives! That evening we showed the *JESUS* Film to over five-hundred at one of the former Communist palace buildings in Krasnyorsk. Many people streamed to the altar for salvation, and we gave each of them a Book of Life.

The next day I went back to prison hospital #18 and showed the *JESUS* Film. Over forty prisoners gave their lives to Jesus. Among them was a man who practiced witchcraft. After hearing the Gospel, he gave me his bag full of wooden squares inscribed with letters which he had used in fortune telling, and readily exchanged Satan's lies for God's truth. Another elderly man had a tube implanted in his throat to breath, and he couldn't speak. But he had heard the message and came forward to accept the Lord.

As we were leaving the institution, the head medical doctor gave me a beautiful ornate wooden box made by one of the prisoners. Inside was a note:

*To Timula, the doctor of souls;
from the doctor of bodies.*

Anatoli Komchaska.

Summer was over, and I could hardly believe that my three-month missionary trip was coming to a close. Before flying back to Moscow, I went to prison #7 one more time to see *"moy druizya,"* (my friends). The Christian prisoners were now holding their own services daily.

Tears welled up in my eyes as I said good-bye. One by one the men came to hug me and thank me for coming. The leader of the group looked at me and said, "I had a vision that Jesus sent you to us." I was humbled.

It was hard for me to leave. Their longing for hope, peace, and joy; their deep sincerity regarding the things of God; and their genuine receptivity to the gospel of Jesus Christ had profoundly affected me. My heart was knit to their hearts. These were my brothers in Christ.

I will never forget the prisoners of Siberia or the Russian Christians. *We* should never forget them!

"When the Son of Man comes in His glory, and all the angels with Him, He will sit on His throne in heavenly glory. All the nations will be gathered before Him, and He will separate the people one from another as a shepherd separates the sheep from the goats. He will put the sheep on His right and the goats on His left."

"Then the King will say to those on His right, 'Come, you who are blessed by my Father; take your inheritance, the kingdom prepared for you since the creation of the world. For I was hungry and you gave me something to eat, I was thirsty and you gave me something to drink, I was a stranger and you invited me in, I needed clothes and you clothed me, I was sick and you looked after me, I was in prison and you came to visit me.'"

"Then the righteous will answer Him, 'Lord, when did we see you hungry and feed you, or thirsty and give you something to drink? When did we see you a stranger and invite you in, or needing clothes and clothe you? When did we see you sick or in prison and go to visit you?'"

"The King will reply, 'I tell you the truth, whatever you did for one of the least of these brethren of Mine, you did for Me!'" [1]

_____

1 Matthew 25:31-40

EPILOGUE

Before returning to the United States, I toured Europe for two months visiting 13 countries by train with a Eurorail pass. From Brussels, Belgium, I faxed a letter to Michelle Durochia thanking her for praying for me and telling her about the awesome things God was doing in Siberia. When I arrived home, we continued to correspond by fax machine. After several months in which we exchanged over a hundred letters, Michelle's roommate accused her of being "in-*fax*-uated." We finally got brave and sent each other a photograph. A couple of weeks later we spoke on the phone for the first time. I was thrilled to hear Michelle tell me in detail about God's call on her life and her love and burden for the Russian people.

In December, 1993, Michelle flew to Washington DC to visit a close family friend and to meet me and my family. I nervously greeted her at the airport with a red rose and a gentle hug. She was beautiful! We had so much fun being together for the next five days we didn't want it to end. When Michelle returned to Vermont for Christmas, I felt empty and was lonely without her.

The day after Christmas I drove to Vermont to be with the woman I had fallen in love with, and to meet her family. From there I drove straight to Springfield, Missouri, to attend the Assemblies of God Theological Seminary. Michelle returned to her secretarial job at Zion Bible Institute in Rhode Island. We continued to fax everyday and talk on the phone, but, we loved and missed each other very much and naturally wanted to be together. In January, after much prayer, Michelle decided to move to Springfield, Missouri, to live and work. Within a short time she was hired as a receptionist/secretary for the National Teen Challenge. We learned more about each other during the next few months and grew deeper in love.

On Thursday, April 14, 1994, I asked Michelle to marry me, and on July 1, we were joined in holy matrimony at her home church in Burlington, Vermont. *"Two are better than one, because they have a good return for their work"* (Ecclesiastes 4:9).

Dear Friend,

If you would like to support the ministry of Tim and Michelle Zello please detach and send the bottom portion of this page. Your prayerful consideration is deeply appreciated.

"For everyone who calls on the name of the Lord will be saved." How, then can they call on the one the one they have not believed in? And how can they believe in the one of whom they have not heard? And how can they hear without someone preaching to them? And how can they preach unless they are sent? For if I preach the gospel, I have nothing to boast of, for necessity is laid upon me; yes, woe is me if I do not preach the gospel (Rom. 10: 13-15; I Cor. 9:16).

Send all correspondence to:

Tim & Michelle Zello
HC-72 Box 1523
Locust Grove, VA 22508

— —

Dear Tim and Michelle,

I will help you reach the unreached with the Gospel as God enables me by sending you (circle one):

$15 $25 $40 $50 $60 $75 $100

or $_____ per month.

Please put me on your mailing list _____(check here).

Enclosed is:
My first monthly gift of $_____.
A one time offering of $_____.

Name: _____
Address: _____
_____

To order additional copies of

Freedom in Siberia

please send $7.95* plus $2.00 shipping and handling to:

Tim Zello
HC-72 Box 1523
Locust Grove, VA 22508

* Quantity discounts available.

For information call (540) 972-0010.